Victorville City Library
15011 Circle Dr
Victorville, CA 92395
760-245-4222

NEVER GIVE IN

Also by Senator Arlen Specter

Passion for Truth

NEVER GIVE IN

BATTLING CANCER IN THE SENATE

Senator Arlen Specter
with Frank J. Scaturro

THOMAS DUNNE BOOKS
ST. MARTIN'S PRESS 🐾 NEW YORK

THOMAS DUNNE BOOKS.
An imprint of St. Martin's Press.

www.thomasdunnebooks.com
www.stmartins.com

ISBN-13: 978-0-312-38306-0
ISBN-10: 0-312-38306-1

First Edition: March 2008

10 9 8 7 6 5 4 3 2 1

This book is dedicated to good friends, Judge Edward R. Becker, Paula Kline, and Carey Lackman, whose stories are told here, and to all other cancer victims who might not have died had the United States government pursued President Nixon's declaration of war against cancer in 1970 with the same intensity as other wars.

Cures for cancer, heart disease, Alzheimer's, Parkinson's, juvenile diabetes, and other deadly diseases are within reach with sufficient funding for medical research by the National Institutes of Health (NIH).

The 110 million Americans who are directly or indirectly affected and the universities and pharmaceutical companies, which benefit from NIH funding, have the political muscle to persuade the federal government to provide enough money to conquer cancer and other maladies.

Contents

ACKNOWLEDGMENTS

One might not think this modest-sized volume relies on the contributions of many people, but it took so many people to make this book what it is that I struggle not to exclude someone. I should begin with special recognition of my family, who have shared my life as well as their recollections of my Hodgkin's battle: my wife, Joan; my sons, Shanin and Steve; Shanin's wife, Tracey; their beautiful daughters, Silvi, Perri, Lilli, and Hatti; my sister and brother-in-law, Hilda and Arthur Morgenstern; my sister, Shirley Kety; and my aunt, Rose Isenberg. I also note five people who not only sat for interviews, but also took the time to review and critique this work as it was in progress: my son Shanin, Dr. John Glick, Charlie Robbins, Evelyn Rosen, and Bettilou Taylor. Dr. Glick showed the same concern for the accuracy of this book's medical content as he did my health. Charlie Robbins provided much helpful background on my 2004 campaign, during which he served on my staff.

Many other individuals generously gave interviews: Todd Averette, Adrienne Baker-Green, Lynda Barness, Chris Bradish, David Brog, Tony Calabro, Don Cohan, Alison Cooper, Jim Cordy, Anthony Cunningham, Captain Michael Curran, David Debruyn, Fran Drescher, William Eskridge, Carl Feldbaum, Steve and Julia Harmelin, Gail and Peter Hearn, Scott Hoeflich, Rich Innes, Juria Jones, Judge Bruce Kasold, Judge Marvin Katz, Evan Kelly, Harold Kim, Tom and Zachary Kline, Jean Larsen, Larry McHugh, Steve Mills, Robert Mueller, Chris Nicholas, Sylvia Nolde, Michael O'Neill, Sudip Parikh, Chris Picaut, Judge Marjorie Rendell, Ed Rosen, Ronald Rotunda, Pop Shenian, Carolyn Short, Gary Slaiman, Captain Ron Smith, Rabbi Jay Stein, Dr. Richard Stoebner, Carrie Stricker, Dr. Scott Trerotola, Adam Turner, Mark Tushnet, David Urban, Andy Wallace, Marie Walton, Dr. Howard Weitz, Tom Worrall, and Jerry and Katie Zucker; former Rep. Billy Tauzin; my Senate colleagues Pat Leahy, Orrin Hatch, Tom Harkin, Lindsay Graham, and Tom Coburn; and President George W. Bush. Many thanks to everyone for taking time out of their busy schedules. My dear friend Judge Edward Becker also graciously gave an interview before his death in spite of his declining health.

Also providing valuable information were Martin Field, Kate Kelly, Hannibal Kemerer, Peter Jensen, and Mark Wilson. Special appreciation goes to our energetic and capable publisher Thomas Dunne, and associate editor Katie Gilligan; and our superb agent Robert Barnett.

Acknowledgments

This undertaking has allowed me to reminisce with
Frank Scaturro and a tape recorder about a recent chapter of my life that I hope can be of encouragement to others who are undergoing illness, as well as their loved ones.
Never give in!

The riders in a race do not stop short when they reach the goal. There is a little finishing canter before coming to a standstill. There is time to hear the kind voices of friends and to say to oneself: The work is done. But just as one says that, the answer comes: "The race is over, but the work never is done while the power to work remains. The canter that brings you to a standstill need not be only coming to rest. It cannot be, while you still live. For to live is to function. That is all there is to living."

And so I end with a line from a Latin poet who uttered the message more than fifteen hundred years ago, "Death plucks my ear and says: Live—I am coming."

—JUSTICE OLIVER WENDELL HOLMES
*Radio broadcast on the occasion
of his ninetieth birthday, March 7, 1931*

NEVER GIVE IN

Preface

I T'S A HELL of a shock to find out you have cancer.

After achieving my lifelong ambition to be chairman of the Judiciary Committee, it looked like the dream had turned into a nightmare. My first thought was How long do I have to live? *What are the chances of survival? Will I be incapacitated and unable to handle my Senate duties, let alone be chairman?*

Then I wondered if the cancer was caused by the tension and stress during the previous year, which was marked by a brutal primary election, a tough general election, and a battle with the far right to get the Judiciary Committee chairmanship. I also wondered if the continuing Senate pressure would aggravate my condition and impede recovery.

Then my thoughts turned to the adequacy of my medical care. My symptoms had appeared for months before any doctor had looked for nodules under my armpits, the tip-off for Hodgkin's lymphoma. It brought back memories, unpleasant memories, from 1979, when one of the nation's leading neurologists had erroneously diagnosed me with ALS, Lou Gehrig's disease. Then I thought of my second death sentence in 1993, when the chief neurosurgeon at Bethesda Naval Hospital looked at an MRI of my skull and said I had a malignant brain tumor and three to six weeks to live. Five years later, a heart double bypass left me with fluid in my lungs, necessitating two more operations and seventeen mostly delirious days in the hospital.

I had survived these misadventures by keeping my cool and focusing on my political duties through all of them. Each time, I had searched for and found doctors who provided the necessary medical expertise. Each time, I had a reservoir of good health and stamina that came from the disciplined conditioning of daily exercise (squash) and a careful diet. Each time, I turned to work, which distracted me from my pain and provided motivation to do my job and recover.

I already had written my autobiography several years ago. It was called *Passion for Truth* and covered some of my career through 2000, just beyond the three score and ten years that biblically marked a lifetime. I have had high aspirations in every phase of my adult life, and my seventies were no exception. If I could control it, the best was yet to come. Yet I did not expect to face the toughest challenges of my Senate career with a health crisis to boot.

Although I have spent a long career communicating

about public issues, I am not practiced in the art of sharing some of the personal details that fill this book. Still, I am encouraged by the hope that some who read this will become better equipped to handle health challenges that face them or their families and friends. I also hope to reduce the number of people who feel impeded by illness from pursuing their calling. Good health is a precious possession that is too often taken for granted. The same is true of the time we have been given to contribute to the world around us. Poor health may limit our time and capacity for achievement, but I firmly believe that vigorous work provides the best way to overcome a health challenge.

Since my own vocation has been public life, there is little of my career I can claim to be my own. That is as it should be. I never allow a day to go by when I take for granted the opportunity I have been given to contribute.

1

The Challenge Before the Challenge

DOES STRESS CAUSE cancer? A November 2005 *New York Times* article considered the connection between stress and cancer an open question but noted "a tenuous connection between stress, the immune system and cancer with a surprising new insight that is changing the direction of research: it now appears that cancer cells make proteins that actually tell the immune system to let them alone and even to help them grow." Women reportedly seemed convinced that stress caused their breast cancer while the "male ego" caused men to view stress as a "sign of weakness" better kept inside.[1] I do not believe in keeping such concerns bottled up, but I also do not believe a challenge should be avoided because it is stressful.

One of my congressional colleagues, former Representative Billy Tauzin, who filled a vacant seat in the House of Representatives in 1980, the same year I was elected to the Senate, is sure that stress and tension caused his cancer. In the summer of 2003, Tauzin relates, he took excessive quantities of Motrin, which caused a bleeding ulcer and inflamed his immune system. He explained his situation to me, saying that stress creates the inflammation of the immune system, which then impedes it from functioning. When the immune system is, in effect, worn out, cancer sets in. He said the bleeding ulcer was diagnosed in December 2003, and a rare intestinal cancer was diagnosed in March 2004. That February he had an operation that removed portions of his stomach, intestines, and pancreas; the cancer had come within a half centimeter of his pancreas. Had the cancer invaded that organ, it most likely would have been fatal, since pancreatic cancer is virtually incurable. Tauzin noted that the operation took out twelve lymph nodes, three of which had dead cancer cells, which indicated that the immune system had successfully fought off some of the cancer attack. His operation, conducted at a very prestigious hospital, did not remove all the cancer, and when he then went to the MD Anderson Cancer Center at the University of Texas, he was told he had a 5 percent chance to survive. He was prescribed a drug known as Avastin, which was off label, meaning it was not designed for his kind of cancer. Miraculously, as he put it, the Avastin normalized his situation and eliminated the need for another operation.

After his treatment, the congressman was advised by

his doctor that he would have to give up his seat in Congress if he was to have any chance of beating the cancer. Following that advice, he did not run for reelection in 2004.

When I met him for lunch in February 2007, he was robust and healthy and working for Pharmaceutical Research and Manufacturers of America (PhRMA). He said he had selected that job because he could help the pharmaceutical industry develop drugs to save other people's lives. Tauzin said that he was diagnosed with a bleeding ulcer in the intestines at the same time that Representative John Dingell, his predecessor as chairman of the Energy and Commerce Committee, who later became chairman after the Democrats gained control in 2006, was diagnosed with a bleeding ulcer in his stomach. Tauzin asserted that beyond any question, both illnesses were the result of stress. After Tauzin had the operation, he was treated with massive doses of chemotherapy. He said his capacity to endure the chemotherapy was considered very surprising by the doctors.

He then disregarded his doctors' advice: He was counseled against exercise, but he drove a tractor or bulldozer on his Louisiana ranch in his effort to regain his physical strength after losing forty-five pounds in his fight with cancer. He undertook that course because he felt that he could beat the cancer only if he regained his strength and stopped losing muscle. He recounted his "fear" every time he would take a CT scan: When he started to feel good, he thought the good cells were returning and was worried that maybe the bad cells were returning as well. When he took a CT scan and got a favorable report, he characterized himself as being euphoric. On one occasion, the doctor was otherwise engaged and took an hour and a half to tell him the favorable results, during which time he was very worried, thinking that the news would be bad. He was much relieved to find the news was good and expressed surprise that the doctor would keep him waiting so long before giving him the news, leading to additional stress. This resembled several of my own experiences with insensitive doctors. During our lunch, however, the former congressman was in his characteristic jovial mood, his health challenge largely behind him and a promising future still ahead.

My own story began in 2004, which promised to be an eventful—and stressful—year. The people of Pennsylvania had never elected anyone to a fifth term in the Senate, and the approaching election promised to add to a list of political challenges I had faced during my public career. With the challenges invariably came excitement, but not always success. Apart from my days in the Air Force (1951–53), my government service dated all the way back to 1959, when I served as an assistant district attorney in Philadelphia. From there, I was elected as district attorney, a Republican in a heavily Democratic city, though not before participating in a dark chapter of history, serving as a member of the staff of the Warren Commission that investigated the assassination of President John F. Kennedy.

In 1967, while serving as district attorney, I ran for mayor of Philadelphia and narrowly lost. Six years later, in 1973, within weeks after the Saturday Night Massacre that cast a cloud over Republican candidates everywhere, I found myself unseated as district attorney in a devastating loss that many thought marked my political demise. Those who would have bet against me for the next five years would have ended up ahead. I made an unsuccessful run for the U.S. Senate in 1976 and for governor in 1978.

But the tide turned in 1980 when I won my first term to the Senate. The three reelection campaigns that followed were successful, but always with an effort—particularly my 1992 general election campaign against Lynn Yeakel. She capitalized on the controversy surrounding my questioning of Professor Anita Hill during the Supreme Court nomination hearings for Clarence Thomas the year before, and polled less than three percentage points behind me. It had been said that I alienated the entire electorate, half by voting against Judge Robert Bork, whose Supreme Court nomination was defeated in 1987 after I led the Judiciary Committee questioning, and the other half by questioning Hill and voting to confirm Thomas.[2] It may be that a senator cannot do his job without angering everyone sometime.

Surviving so many potentially career-ending challenges left me confident I could win tough battles. Nowadays, getting renominated by one's party is usually not a tremendous struggle for senators, and incumbents routinely win primary election contests. To be sure, there have been and will continue to be exceptions. In 2002, Representative John Sununu defeated incumbent Bob Smith of New Hampshire in that state's Republican primary, but Smith had alienated many Republicans by bolting the party to run for president, only to return to it soon after. In 2006, incumbent Joe Lieberman of Connecticut would be defeated in a bitter Democratic primary based on his support for the war in Iraq.

In 2004, I was the only sitting senator to face a primary. In retrospect, after the Hodgkin's diagnosis, I wonder if the stressful, intense primary campaign caused or contributed to the cancer. The reelection campaign was challenging because of my long track record as a centrist Republican in an increasingly polarized environment—one in which power has seemingly shifted to the extreme ideological base of each party, with potentially dire consequences for the elected official who does not meet the criteria of activists on the far ends of the political spectrum. This polarization created a stressful environment for the primary.

This situation was something of a break from the past. Among Republican incumbents, I was perhaps the last of a group of centrists that once included Mark Hatfield and Bob Packwood of Oregon, Bob Stafford of Vermont, Lowell Weicker of Connecticut, Bill Cohen of Maine, John Chafee of Rhode Island, Warren Rudman of New Hampshire, Alan Simpson of Wyoming, Jack Danforth of Missouri, Charles Percy of Illinois, Charles Mathias of Maryland, and my colleague from Pennsylvania, John Heinz.[3] Others had since taken their place—Lincoln Chafee of

Rhode Island, Gordon Smith of Oregon, and Maine senators Olympia Snowe and Susan Collins readily come to mind—but there is no doubt the ranks of the centrists have been diminishing. Linc, as we called the younger Chafee, would be defeated in the November 2006 election.

What was true in so much of the country was reflected in Pennsylvania. In April 2004, the *Los Angeles Times* observed, "Though Pennsylvania has a history of electing centrist Republicans, such as former Governor Tom Ridge and the late Senator John Heinz, that is changing."[4] As a *Wall Street Journal* column noted, "Republican primaries used to hinge heavily on the four big suburban Philadelphia counties." This had changed as the party's growth occurred "west and north of that region—Lancaster and York and Lehigh Counties."[5] My first Senate victory began with a successful challenge to Harold "Bud" Haabestad, the state Republican chairman and Princeton basketball star who was the choice of the statewide Republican leadership, in the 1980 primary. Nearly a quarter century later, a parallel challenge would be launched, only this time *I* was the organization's choice.

Like modern races for the presidency, the 2004 primary campaign began well before its official start. A three-term member of the House of Representatives, Patrick J. Toomey of the Lehigh Valley, had first been elected in 1998 with the promise he would limit himself to three terms, many political observers thinking he was planning a Senate run in 2004 from the start. Aware that he could pose a formidable challenge, the only prudent course for me was to prepare for a tough campaign.

Being reasonably certain Toomey was going to run against me, I started my 2004 campaign for reelection on November 6, 2002, the day after he won his third term. Starting at 9:00 A.M., I was on the phone for two full days calling the seventy key Republicans in his district. The results were excellent, with sixty-eight agreeing to support me, one equivocating, and only one negative response. Those numbers later slipped, but I was satisfied I had done my homework in the Lehigh Valley, as I had throughout the state for more than two decades.

In 1980, I was the first statewide candidate to make a point of visiting all sixty-seven counties and publicizing it. I continued the practice by visiting each county once a year, in addition to multiple visits to the metropolitan areas. I found this method indispensable in becoming acquainted with the complex issues of 12 million constituents with diverse interests in agriculture, steel, coal, and timber, not to mention the problems of the cities, veterans, and senior citizens. Once I started, I found campaigning fun despite the hard work involved. That was a good thing, because Representative Toomey would not let me win with anything short of my best efforts.

My position on the Appropriations Committee enabled me to secure significant federal projects throughout Pennsylvania. I had mounted strong campaigns for reelection in 1986, 1992, and 1998, based on my seniority on the committee. From 1998 through 2002, I had visited the Lehigh Valley twenty-eight times and become aware of the need for federal assistance for universities, hospitals, highways, businesses, law enforcement, and other local needs. In 2004, I emphasized I was second in line to become chairman, a position no Pennsylvanian ever had held. Combining this theme with my established independence, my campaign slogan was "Courage. Clout. Conviction." Thirty-five years had not changed my approach much from 1969, when I ran for reelection as district attorney alongside Tom Gola, the city controller candidate, with the slogan, "They're Tougher, They're Younger, and Nobody Owns Them." The only thing that really had changed was the unchangeable: No one can stay young.

Representative Toomey found my record and campaign tailor-made for his contrary approach. His ultra-conservative economic philosophy had led him to oppose increases in federal assistance even where it involved projects in his own district that were federally funded elsewhere. This may have contributed to his sluggish record on constituent service, while I prided myself on an approach that once led Senator Heinz quizzically to ask a staffer: "How is it Arlen Specter gets there the day before the flood?" The Wall Street–oriented Club for Growth favored deep tax cuts and deeper cuts in federal spending, a popular platform for a Republican primary. This group, the fifth-largest 527 political organization at the time,[6] made Toomey their poster boy with a highly successful national fund-raising campaign. The Club for Growth was so closely coordinated with Toomey's personal campaign organization that I called it the "club for Toomey," a virtual wholly owned subsidiary of his campaign. Indeed, Toomey would later take over as the group's president and CEO.

My second major campaign theme brought out the greatest impact I would have during another term in the Senate: Because Senator Orrin Hatch had to step down due to term limits, I was in line to become chairman of the Judiciary Committee after serving as a member of that committee for all of my twenty-four years in the Senate. As Pennsylvania's first popularly elected four-term senator, I would become the first senator from my state since 1833 to chair that important committee. This prospect played right into the hands of my primary opposition as it motivated the right to target me.

A fight with the ultra–right wing of the party had been in the making for some time. It was no secret that there were some stark differences between us, but that is not to overlook the natural desire of political leaders, on or off the campaign cycle, to reach out and seek common ground with others. Early on, I met with the founder of the Club for Growth and participated in one of the group's sessions, though it obviously never became an ally. In the spring of 2003, I had lunch in the Senate dining room with Reverend Jerry Falwell, causing *The Washington Post* to surmise I was posturing in reaction to my primary challenger.[7] The meal was actually a straightforward discussion of our mutual support for Israel and for sexual abstinence programs and our differences on the issue of stem cell research, all of which had been our views for years. Falwell, to my knowledge, remained uninvolved in the primary.

Later that year, however, I did have another lunch—this time with Steve Freind, an outspoken opponent of abortion who ran a primary against me in 1992—for the principal purpose of expanding support. An endorsement was not forthcoming, but I appreciated Freind's honesty: "If Pat Toomey was pro-abort, I would be with you," he remarked. "You know how important the issue is. I can't be with you."

Indeed, a phalanx of pro-life activists converged upon Pennsylvania to campaign against me, led by Dr. James Dobson, head of the organization Focus on the Family and a worldwide radio program of the same name. Dobson left Colorado Springs, home of his media empire, to travel to conservative Lancaster County to denounce me. These opponents saw a second term by President George W. Bush as the opportunity to confirm new Supreme Court justices to reverse *Roe v. Wade,* the landmark case that established a woman's right to choose to terminate her pregnancy. Notwithstanding my support for President Bush's reelection and my votes in favor of all his judicial nominees to date, they were concerned that I, as a pro-choice senator, would oppose pro-life nominees to the Supreme Court, which in turn would undercut their three-decade campaign to reverse *Roe.*

The Toomey camp even recruited Judge Bork. What made my opponent's campaign so unusually potent was its widespread support among Republican primary voters who desperately wanted to reverse *Roe* and cut taxes along with federal spending. Toomey campaigned as the pro-life alternative to me, though he had initially run for the House as a pro-choice candidate in 1998, when he found himself running against multiple pro-life primary opponents.[8] Toomey also had served as a cochairman of my campaign finance committee in 2001 before he announced against me.

Personally, Toomey was a bright, articulate, well-groomed, youthful candidate (age forty-two on primary day) who was earnest in his delivery if a tad humorless. An Eagle Scout before age fifteen and cum laude graduate of Harvard, he was astutely described by *The Philadelphia Inquirer* as a "conservative with a moderate demeanor."[9] On a certain level, I could respect his deep devotion to fiscal conservatism in his own backyard, even though I felt it was not in the best interests of Pennsylvania. However, I knew that the issues that made him attractive to Republican primary voters likely would bring him defeat in the general election.

President Bush and Senator Rick Santorum knew this too and backed my candidacy solidly and early. In February 2003, the White House sent a warning shot to Toomey by sending Chief of Staff Andy Card to host a fund-raiser for me in the congressman's home district. The president, Vice-President Dick Cheney, and even First Lady Laura Bush campaigned for me in Pennsylvania, where they would tout such themes as my support for administration initiatives in the war on terror, tax cuts, and judicial nominations. Always gracious about his support, the president would say of me, "He doesn't owe me anything except good government." I had developed a cordial relationship with him during the 2000 campaign and his first three years in office, and got to know him very well in 2004 when I traveled with him on Air Force One.

That year, the president had his own reelection to worry about, and Pennsylvania was an important state in his contest with Senator John Kerry, the Democratic nominee. During his first term and reelection campaign, President Bush visited Pennsylvania more than forty times, and I accompanied him on most of those trips. We discussed at some length the Judiciary Committee chairman's role, and I told the president he was preeminently fair in asking for a commitment from the chairman to conduct prompt hearings on those he nominated for judgeships, and then report the nominations to the floor for up-or-down votes by the full Senate.

The president did not skirt my reputation for independence when he spoke to crowds. He told one audience in Ardmore, Pennsylvania, "Oh, he doesn't do everything you ask him to do all the time"—at which point the audience chuckled—"but when you need him . . . when you need him, he's there."[10] George W. Bush has a disarming but wry sense of humor that surfaced when I flew with him to a conference on education and the economy in Harrisburg on February 12, 2004, my seventy-fourth birthday. He acknowledged me to the gathered crowd as Pennsylvania's "senior senator," but added, "I try to downplay the senior part."[11] During a later trip to Scranton, we landed in Air Force One as it was drizzling outside. I was wearing my trench coat and did not expect the president to invite me out onto the airplane steps, but he did. He exited the plane first but spotted my coat as I stood on his right. "Arlen, Arlen," he quipped, "we're going to have to upgrade your wardrobe." I told my son Shanin the story, and he bought me a more presentable raincoat.

Campaigns are full of surprises, and a real highlight on the campaign trail was seeing my old friend, former Senate majority leader Bob Dole, who came in February for an entire day of events in the Lehigh Valley and Scranton areas. During his over twenty-seven years in the Senate, Dole represented Kansas, where I spent my early life. When I moved from Wichita to Russell in 1942 at the age of twelve, Dole, then nineteen, was a big wheel on the University of Kansas basketball team. He was once a much older man, but in these intervening years, I have pretty much caught up with him. He has an extraordinary sense of humor, which, unfortunately, rarely surfaced during his presidential run in 1996. We frequently talked about his experience as Russell's county attorney compared to my work as Philadelphia's district attorney. When he returned home to Russell as a wounded war veteran, both parties wanted him to run on their ticket. Although his family was Democratic, he was not on record for one party or the other. As he tells the story, he checked the registration and found out there were twice as many Republicans in Russell County as Democrats and decided he was a Republican. (In contrast, I had swum upstream, changing my registration to Republican in an overwhelmingly Democratic city.) Dole always liked to emphasize the small town values of integrity, a strong work ethic, and family that life in Russell instilled in its residents. On the trail for me in 2004, he remarked to a reporter regarding my political reputation, "You can't be rigid in your views and get anything done for the people of your state."[12] There is a lot of truth to that, and I believe that is one reason so many elected officials, including the Senate leadership and all but two members of Pennsylvania's delegation to the House (who remained neutral), endorsed my campaign. Much of the party rank and file saw the matter differently, which made it a contest.

The campaign required every bit of energy that had propelled my twenty-four years of constituent travel and Washington service, not to mention a frenetic schedule. My formal, two-day statewide campaign announcement tour began on January 8, 2004, with a squash match at 6:45 A.M., then a 9:00 announcement at the National Constitution Center in Philadelphia, a flight to Harrisburg for an 11:45 news conference at the state capitol, a flight to Pittsburgh for a 2:45 announcement, a flight to Erie for a 5:15 announcement, followed by a flight to State College, where I had dinner and spent the night.

Between campaign events and official events, day - after day I often had a dozen or more stops—a phenomenon my campaign manager, Chris Nicholas, called

"Specterpalooza." My schedule was filled with meetings with innumerable segments of the population—manufacturing, medical, agricultural, law enforcement, veterans; the list goes on—and media appearances and phone drives in between. There was not a moment to waste, but also not a person to take for granted. I was once reminded I walked up fifteen rows in Veterans Stadium to shake a hand (I wasn't keeping track). Because I want to know what is on everyone's mind, I prefer to deliver short speeches—ten to twelve minutes for a typical group, five minutes for town meetings—before turning to questions from the audience for the bulk of the program. No audience is too small to merit the same attention that goes to the larger ones. The 2004 primary campaign did not break any personal records for small crowds. I recall a campaign event at a Philadelphia home in 1965, when I ran for district attorney, in which only one person showed up to meet Jim Cavanaugh, who ran for city controller, and me. I gave a short speech, and Cavanaugh followed with his own unabridged lengthy talk.

Thanks to technology that many take for granted today, I could conduct media interviews by car or cell phone while riding around the state. As during my non-campaign season, I remained a regular on the *Michael Smerconish Morning Show,* a news talk radio program based in Philadelphia, and Angelo Cataldi's sports radio show, which has long allowed me the enjoyment of commenting on my local sports teams while making contact with many listeners beyond the news and political show audience. Talk shows like Cataldi's provided a diversion (albeit a politically constructive one) to the political events that saturated my schedule.

The experience of campaigning was the most fun when family members joined me. My wife, Joan, typically accompanied me on my weekend campaign travels. A beautiful, stately woman of tremendous poise, she is a distinguished personage in her own right—a former four-term city councilwoman presently involved in development (fund-raising) for the Constitution Center in Philadelphia. She dresses as if she just stepped out of *Vogue*, and the crowds love to see her. When she is around, I have someone to speak with between campaign stops, and she always has constructive comments about my speeches.

I was also joined at key events by my son Shanin, his wife Tracey, and their two older daughters, Silvi and Perri. During my announcement tour, Perri, aged eight, amused Joan and me no end at a particular stop in Harrisburg. After observing my routine at the Constitution Center, our first stop, she realized in Harrisburg, our second stop, that I would make another speech after she viewed Joan and me shaking hands. She walked up to the podium, pulled up a chair (which was quite a chore for her), stood on top of it, took the microphone, and delivered a speech. "Vote for Arlen" was her refrain. (I am the only grandparent the girls refer to by first name, at my insistence.) Then she did the same at our next stop, Pittsburgh. After we moved on to Erie, she began a new routine, dancing on the stage as I spoke to the crowd. I preferred the spontaneity of the moment to sticking with the campaign's set program. Everyone found the performance funny, and that was where much of the crowd's attention was directed.

During an August trip to Erie, Silvi, aged ten, accompanied me on the bus with the president, Mrs. Bush, and their two daughters, Jenna and Barbara. Laura Bush, always in touch with children, swapped stories with third-grader Silvi about her experiences teaching the third grade. After the photos of the trip returned, the president inscribed a picture of him with Silvi that now hangs proudly in my outer office. Silvi returned for a photo with the president at the 2006 Christmas ball, then a young lady of almost thirteen. To the extent I could, I have taken my granddaughters to the White House summer picnics and tours, as well as to other political activities, to give them a feel for politics and government.

Our two sons, Shanin and Steve, were involved in my political activities from an early age. A particular moment always comes to mind from when I ran for district attorney in 1965. My press secretary called at 11:00 P.M. the night before the primary, saying that Joan and I should come to the polls promptly at 7:00 A.M. in order to make the early edition of *The Philadelphia Bulletin*. Joan and I looked at each other wondering what to do with Shanin, seven, and Steve, four, since it was obviously too late to get a 6:30 A.M. babysitter the next day, so we brought the children with us that morning. Since Joan and I were registered Democrats and I was running in the Republican primary, I urged her not to vote for any candidate, because we did not want to be accused of trying to influence the Democratic election. So she voted only on the questions on the ballot. When she was unable to extricate herself from the polling booth, we found that the curtain would not open if the voter did not vote for at least one of the candidates. Steve, who was waiting for her outside the booth, panicked when his mother was trapped inside. When she finally came out, a wonderful, warm family reunion materialized. That brought a big smile to my face, which was hard to do at that stage of my political career. A photo depicting the scene appeared above the fold of the afternoon *Bulletin*.

My cell phone enabled me to keep in touch with family members who were farther away. My older sisters Hilda and Shirley, along with Hilda's husband Arthur, resided in New Jersey, and my Aunt Rose has lived in Wichita, Kansas, the city of my birth, since before I was born. In fact, Aunt Rose was with her sister, my mother, when she gave birth to me and is responsible for my name. After my parents announced I would be named Abraham after my paternal grandfather, Avram, Aunt Rose said, "you're not going to do that to this poor little baby." She suggested instead the surname of her favorite actor, Richard Arlen.[13] That has not stopped her from continuing to call me by my boyhood nickname, "Boozy Boy." A close family friend had given his son, Danny Greenberg, born sixteen months before me, the nickname "Sonny Boy" after the Al Jolson song of that title, and my father adopted the variation "Boozy Boy" for me. Aunt Rose, in her nineties by 2004, was as spirited as ever and oversaw me with the devotion of a mother. Over the years, I have made it a practice to call my family frequently, as they have always been my biggest cheerleaders. Among their significant contributions, they have traveled tirelessly throughout Pennsylvania campaigning for me.

I am fortunate that my campaigns have inspired my entire political household. Between my campaign staff, official staff as volunteers on their own time, and fund-raising staff, I was fortunate to have a devoted and talented group working with me. Sylvia Nolde was an astute and dedicated staffer and adviser since my first year in the Senate, when I inherited her as my scheduler from outgoing Senator Jacob Javits of New York. One day, after being in the Senate for about eight weeks, I called her at 5:52 P.M. saying I would miss the 6:00 P.M. Metroliner. She told me to hurry to the station because she could hold the train for five minutes, a trick she learned from her time with Javits. Meanwhile, Senator Joe Biden of Delaware, elected in 1972, was racing past me to the gate when a conductor, not knowing who he was, shouted: "Slow down, Bud, there's a senator coming." Biden tracked me down on the train, almost irate, to ask me how I found out in eight weeks how to hold the train when he had not made that discovery in eight years. That was the first of many long train rides together. During the 2004 campaign, Sylvia would be a key operative in my campaign organization, Citizens for Arlen Specter.

Todd Averette and Alison Cooper, who had worked on

my Senate staff, were in charge of fund-raising. They could accurately be called young veterans, thirty-somethings who personified attentiveness to one's work, and who knew how to maintain a harmonious staff. Alison had started on my staff as a receptionist in 1994 and would finish in 2006 as my chief of staff. Another former staffer in the campaign household was the genial David Urban, who held a number of positions in my office over the years, including chief of staff, and excelled at each of them. Carey Lackman, who served as my chief of staff through the primary—one of the first women to serve in that capacity in the Senate—had been with me for all but two years since 1991.

When the Senate was in session, I spent most weekdays in Washington to conduct Senate business. Mondays and Fridays typically allowed me to spend at least some time in Pennsylvania. Besides constituent casework and my Judiciary Committee membership, my responsibilities entailed chairing the Veterans Affairs Committee and the Appropriations Subcommittee on Labor, Health and Human Services, and Education. The latter assignment entails management of federal spending in a variety of areas, including public health. I had long tried to champion the government's role in exploring the frontiers of medicine in order to save lives, and this mission became closer to my heart as I witnessed Carey Lackman struggle with breast cancer throughout the primary season. Few on the staff had any idea how ill she was, and her work ethic and personal strength did much to conceal it.

Even with this skilled team, the race intensified as primary day approached, and I worried that too many Republicans would not vote out of a lack of awareness of how serious a chance I had of losing. I knew I was in trouble from day one, and unsurprisingly, the race increasingly became a negative one. The Toomey campaign's basic strategy entailed a persistent attack on me as a "liberal." The *National Review* provided a forum for my opponent, coming to his aid with a vitriolic September 2003 cover story headline, "The Worst Republican Senator: Why Pennsylvania Should Get Rid of Arlen Specter."[14] In response, my campaign procured a letter from the three former and the current Republican Senate majority leaders—Howard Baker, Bob Dole, Trent Lott, and Bill Frist—calling me "one of the best Senators in promoting Republican values and policies." A Toomey ad charged that "nearly 70 percent of the time," I "voted the same way" as John Kerry: "And that makes Arlen Specter 100 percent too liberal." Those numbers, drawn from votes cast in 2002, omitted to mention that Kerry voted with President Bush 72 percent of the time.

In mid-April 2004, *Wall Street Journal* columnist Al Hunt ran a column about the campaign entitled, "Down and Nasty in the Keystone State." Hunt remarked about me, "While he has made a legislative mark on important national issues—medical research most notably—he is a prodigious producer of pork and unsurpassed in constituency services."[15] The "pork" charge was a cornerstone of the Toomey campaign. My biggest challenge, in fact, was less my opponent than my own record, which a solid majority of Pennsylvanians approved except for the very-right-wing Republicans. Still, I find one of the best ways as an incumbent to deflect ill-considered criticism is to put the critic in my shoes. I unabashedly defended what I call "bringing home the bacon"[16] and challenged Representative Toomey to share with the public what federal spending *in Pennsylvania* he would criticize as wasteful. For days, my opponent was unresponsive until his campaign came up with a single expenditure—an $800,000 outhouse in a national park that was finished two years before he was elected to Congress.[17]

Terry Madonna, director of Franklin and Marshall College's Keystone Poll, observed, "Arlen always wins ugly."[18] There was some truth to this, and in more ways than one. A little over a month before the primary election, I tripped on a sidewalk defect and fell flat on my face as I left the Tangerine Restaurant in Philadelphia on a Saturday night. I went to the emergency room of Jefferson Hospital and was visibly bruised, with two shiners and a split lower lip. I was scheduled to appear on national television—CNN's *Late Edition with Wolf Blitzer*—the next day.

To hell with it, I thought; I may as well go forward on the show in full glory. Blitzer asked me about my injury on the air, and I explained, "Came down hard on my lip, Wolf. I tripped on a defect in the sidewalk and got a little bump, but I'm feeling OK."

The bruises worsened, and by Monday, I had become an absolute mess, but I attended a scheduled farm event in western Pennsylvania with Governor Ed Rendell, which was shown on C-SPAN. I had something to say on Sunday on CNN, on Monday on the farm, and Tuesday on the Senate floor, so I said it notwithstanding my appearance. It would be the same months later when I appeared for my Senate business pallid, skinny, and bald while undergoing a chemotherapy treatment.

Charlie Robbins, my communications director, said I looked as if I had gone ten rounds with Mike Tyson. *Roll Call,* the Capitol Hill newspaper, reported on my activities that Tuesday: "Senate tongues were wagging big-time on Tuesday night when Specter rose to give a speech on the Senate floor and showed off a busted lip, two black eyes and a scary-looking nose. (This, of course, was not the first occasion that the infamously testy Specter has had his nose out of joint—at least not figuratively.)"[19]

Jokes aside, the race, as feared, tightened as primary day approached. In January 2004, polls had me with a 23-point lead over Toomey, which dropped to a 15-point lead on April 7 and a 5-point lead on April 20, a week before the primary.[20] My opponent's negative surge was apparently the result of his blitz of campaign commercials, which worked enough for him to come out ahead among self-identified conservatives by April 20—a reversal of my previous lead among conservatives. Realizing the margin would be razor-thin, I pressed for every last vote I could get. Toomey was doing an effective job of reaching out to the base, and many were surprised to hear how close the contest was.

Of course, the only poll that counted was the actual primary election, which occurred on April 27. It was a day fraught with suspense. At the time I voted that morning in Philadelphia, voter turnout appeared to be low in the southeastern part of the state, which fed my team's long-standing anxiety over the effects of little turnout. Several campaign staffers went to pray for victory at the Convent of Divine Love, the home of cloistered nuns known as the "pink sisters," who invite prayers in times of difficulty.

That evening, the campaign camped out at the Bellevue-Stratford Hotel in Philadelphia as the numbers came in. I arrived looking exhausted, according to my staff, but I did not sense more than the usual fatigue of a tough campaign. I went to the ballroom, where numerous cameras and reporters were assembled. I went from camera to camera telling the voters very directly in the live 6:00 P.M. news shows that the election could be decided by a few votes. KYW, Philadelphia's most widely listened-to news radio program, gave me three minutes live shortly after 7:00 P.M. to state my case. My constituents knew how I had served the state for twenty-three years, I said, and if they wanted me to continue, please come to the polls and demonstrate their support.

After the polls closed, several hundred supporters gathered in the ballroom. A smaller group of about seventeen people occupied a computer-filled war room off to the side, where returns were being tracked. There Joan, Shanin, Tracey, Shanin's friend and law partner Tom Kline, and Tom's wife, Paula, joined several campaign and Senate staffers around a large table, where everyone was mulling over numbers as they came in. The experience was an emotional roller coaster. At one point, a 95,000-vote error from Bucks County gave me a reported 59 to 41 percent edge. The jump startled several of us. What happened? Tel Aviv must have come in, joked my campaign treasurer, Steve Harmelin. Once the error was discovered, the margin shrank to 51 to 49 percent, then further to a fifty-fifty statistical tie. There was great concern over the last returns to be reported, which would come from rural conservative areas that were thought to be leaning toward Toomey. The situation appeared so bleak that several staffers were convinced I had lost. Some even began to formulate their farewells, telling their coworkers it had been nice working together. When three returns came in, however, my team was elated to find I had carried those areas—some in greater numbers than the suburban regions typically considered my areas of strength.

Notwithstanding that pleasant surprise, my lead continued to shrink. I sat next to my pollster, Glen Bolger, who was analyzing the narrowing race, with the total vote yet uncounted. My anxiety, still high, was eased substantially as Bolger told me Toomey would have to get a very high percentage of the outstanding vote in order to overcome my narrow lead. As the lead shrank, so did the number of outstanding, unreported votes. I do not recall Bolger's precise comments, but with a small number of outstanding votes, he said something to the effect that Toomey would have to get 70 percent of the remainder. And then a few minutes later, with the lead even closer but fewer votes outstanding, he said Toomey would have to get something like 80 percent of the remainder. I derived considerable solace as the lead narrowed, because it seemed highly unlikely that Toomey could get enough of the remaining votes to take the lead, which he never did.

Watching the election returns for the tension-filled 2004 primary was vastly different from my narrow loss for mayor in 1967. My pollster at the time, John Bucci, worked for Philadelphia's KYW radio on election night and would take a few sample returns, compare them to previous elections, and make a projection. He did that a few minutes after the polls closed on the mayoral election. At about 8:15 or 8:20, while Joan and I were dressing, preparing to go to election headquarters, Shanin, then ten, walked into the bedroom and said, "Daddy, John Bucci says you lost." It was an abrupt, decisive end to a vigorous, sometimes violent campaign.

Now the final tally showed the numbers at 50.8 percent to 49.2 percent; I had eked out a 1.6 percent victory, with a margin of 17,146 votes out of 1,044,532 cast. It was not until about 1:00 A.M. that Toomey called me to concede. Our phone call was brief, but my opponent was gracious in congratulating me on the victory. After he spoke to his supporters, I spoke to mine in Bellevue-Stratford's ballroom: "I compliment Congressman Pat Toomey on a hard-fought campaign. Now is the time, having settled our family disagreement within the Republican Party, to unify, to re-elect President Bush, to maintain the Republican majority in the United States Senate." A good portion of the crowd had left, but I was pleased to see about half, numbering 150 or so, remained to the end.

It was a bittersweet moment for my friends and for me, for reasons beyond those visible to the viewing public. Carey, who had taken off the last several weeks after a long streak without missing a day of work, spent the entire primary night with the team, but she was in tremendous pain. She was not up to taking part in all the cheers and hugs that followed the victory announcement, but she stood behind me as I gave my victory speech—despite her difficulty standing at any length that evening. I was not alone in thinking this would be her last campaign. She had fought cancer tenaciously years earlier, but the illness returned, too aggressive to overcome—and, in my view, preventable. She died less than three months after the primary—four days after getting married, wheelchair-bound, in the chapel of the Georgetown University Hospital. She was a statuesque blonde, personable, a brilliant and studious leader who was a mentor to the young staff. I could always trust her to handle the issues that cascaded into the office with aplomb, dignity, and efficiency.

I visited her home the night before she died. Carey was propped up in a hospital bed that had been brought to her home, yet she looked radiant. I thought it was beautiful she had just been married. Our most prominent memory at that moment was our work to expand health care research. Over the years, we had striven to increase funding for the National Institutes of Health (NIH), the nation's principal vehicle for such research. Holding her hand, I told her that she and I had led that fight and that I would continue our work. She spoke softly when she could, and she said she was at peace with herself, fully aware of her imminent fate. Her words said it all about the type of person she was: "I've had a good run." She was forty-eight.

2

THE AUTUMN OF MY CAREER

THE 2004 PRIMARY had been the most difficult election of my Senate career, even more so than the 1992 general election against Lynn Yeakel, which Carl Feldbaum, my chief of staff at the time, noted was "so hard it could crack a diamond." Nonetheless, the roller coaster of 2004 would not end with the primary. I was in for a fall season like no other. It began with the general election campaign, which on the surface seemed anticlimactic next to what preceded it, but was still more difficult than the races of most of my colleagues. Again, the tension and pressure were front and center. This was another fact that, after my cancer diagnosis, made me wonder how much, if at all, the stress factor caused or contributed to the cancer. To begin, the primary had cost my entire campaign chest, $15 million. We had to devote all the resources we could to that contest, because as Steve

Harmelin noted, there would be no general election unless we won the primary. That also meant, however, we had to raise funds all over again to finance the November race.

There had been rumors through early 2003 that TV talk show host Chris Matthews was considering a run for the Democratic nomination to the Senate from Pennsylvania, but he ultimately decided against it. The Democratic Senatorial Campaign Committee (DSCC), which works to promote Democratic candidates nationally for the Senate, established an Arlen Specter Watch in Pennsylvania to track my votes and actions in 2003. The Democrats hoped for a Toomey win in the primary, for the same reason many Republicans hoped to see the incendiary former Vermont governor Howard Dean become the Democratic nominee for president. But in fact, the DSCC probably bolstered my Republican support when it criticized me as President Bush's "Enabler in Chief."

By happenstance, my November opponent was a member of the so-called "Dean Dozen," a slate of candidates (numbering actually more than a dozen) who were endorsed by Dean's political action committee. The Democratic candidate for the Senate, Representative Joe Hoeffel, had entered the House the same year as Pat Toomey but was as different ideologically as one could imagine. Perhaps the most notable episode during his campaign was his arrest, along with two other congressmen, for trespassing while protesting human rights violations in front of the Sudanese embassy.

Much of the general election mirrored the presidential election's debate over the war in Iraq. Representative Hoeffel had voted to authorize force in Iraq, but became a harsh critic of the administration's conduct prior to the start of the military campaign in March 2003. Like Senator Kerry, his initial vote of support for the war was coupled with a vote against funding it, which in my view ran away from our commitment. As doubt was cast on the existence of weapons of mass destruction (WMDs) in Iraq prior to the invasion, Hoeffel bluntly accused the administration of lying to bring the country into war. Much as I have shared and publicly expressed concerns about intelligence failures, I took issue with overblown rhetoric that overlooked a difficult decision the president took in good faith to respond to Saddam Hussein's persistent violation of numerous U.N. resolutions requiring compliance with inspections for prohibited WMDs.[1]

With the benefit of improved (if not quite twenty-twenty) hindsight, my view was that had we known there were no WMDs in Iraq, we would not have gone in to remove Saddam's regime from power. Having done so, however, we could not leave that country in chaos. When Saddam was captured in December 2003, I expressed my view that he should be tried at The Hague, where a war crimes tribunal already was established. The Hague idea fell flat, in part because the tribunal did not impose a death penalty, a point on which the Toomey campaign capitalized in order to ridicule the idea. Still, I thought that Saddam should be brought to trial swiftly, because when the world learned the details of his despicable slaughter of thousands of innocent Iraqis, his use of chemicals on his own people, and his plundering of the nation's treasury, people everywhere would collectively say good riddance.

In the spring of 2004, while riding in the presidential limousine on a campaign trip in Pennsylvania, I urged the president to bring Saddam to trial as soon as possible. He then asked, "Would you be willing to handle the prosecution personally?" Immodestly thinking of Supreme Court Justice Robert H. Jackson, who took a leave of absence after World War II to try Nazi war criminals, I said yes.

"Well, I was just kidding," he replied.

"Well, I wasn't," I shot back. When I placed a call to U.S. personnel working with the provisional government in Baghdad, I discovered that neither a trial court nor an appellate court had been established, so a prompt trial was not possible. That issue would have to wait to be resolved.

The general election campaign, rigorous on all sides, included a right-wing Constitution Party candidate whose support came from a contingent of Toomey supporters. On election day, November 2, I won 53 to 42 percent, with 4 percent going to the Constitution Party candidate, at the same time President Bush lost Pennsylvania to Senator Kerry by 2.5 percent while winning nationally. I felt a great weight lifted from my shoulders with the passing of my year's two political challenges. I celebrated this victory with my family and supporters at the Four Seasons Hotel in Philadelphia, where the theme from *Rocky* played as I took the stage to thank the crowd.

Not long after departing the stage, I joined the victory party with a martini in each hand and what staffers described as a boyish grin on my face. "Specter Wins Fifth Term After Tough Year" read the Associated Press headline on my victory. As it turned out, it was premature to close the book on the year 2004. It was, after all, only November.

The major obstacles were behind me, and there seemed to be no question about the chairmanship that awaited me. Under the Republican Conference Rules, I was senior in line for the position, having served in the Senate for twenty-four years and on the Judiciary Committee the entire time. The rules did technically require an affirmative vote by a majority of the Republican members of the committee, with ratification by the full Senate Republican Conference (as Republican members of the Senate were collectively known), but those provisions were regarded as mere formalities. They had never been used to reject an incoming chairman.

The morning after the election, following a pleasant breakfast with my sisters and their families, I held a traditional day-after news conference at about 11:30 A.M. at the Four Seasons Hotel that had hosted our victory party. I felt a certain euphoria from the night before, and I allowed the press conference to run on.

Little did I know that it was at that point that the most difficult, tension-filled campaign began: to win the chairmanship of the Senate Judiciary Committee. The questions turned to judicial nominations and the future of the Supreme Court. This was a sore topic, because

Senate Democrats had defeated a number of President Bush's lower-court nominees with filibusters—legislative maneuvers to extend debate in order to prevent a vote from ever taking place—and there was widespread concern over how a Supreme Court nomination might play out. A reporter asked me, "Mr. Bush, he just won the election, even with the popular vote as well. If he wants anti-abortion judges up there, you are caught in the middle of it, what are you going to do?"

I replied:

When you talk about judges who would change the right of a woman to choose, overturn *Roe v. Wade,* I think that is unlikely. And I have said that bluntly during the course of the campaign and before. When the *Inquirer* endorsed me, they quoted my statement that *Roe v. Wade* was inviolate. And that 1973 decision, which has been in effect now for 33 years, was buttressed by the 1992 decision [*Planned Parenthood v. Casey*], written by three Republican justices—O'Connor, Souter, and Kennedy—and nobody can doubt Anthony Kennedy's conservativism or pro-life position, but that's the fabric of the country. Nobody can be confirmed today who didn't agree with *Brown v. Board of Education* on integration, and I believe that while you traditionally do not ask a nominee how they're going to decide a specific case, there's a doctrine and a fancy label term, *stare decisis*: precedent, which I think protects that issue. That is my view, now, before, and always.

The reporter followed, "You are saying the President should not bother or make the move to send somebody up there who is clearly anti-abortion?" I answered:

I don't want to prejudge what the President is going to do. But the President is well aware of what happened when a number of his nominees were sent up, with the filibuster, and the President has said he is not going to impose a litmus test, he faced that issue squarely in the third debate and I would not expect the President, I would expect the President to be mindful of the considerations that I mentioned.

These comments seemed innocuous to me at the time—a statement of fact that was difficult to dispute, albeit on a contentious issue. Both Chris Nicholas, who looked forward to the postcampaign wind-down, and my new chief of staff, David Brog, breathed a sigh of relief that the press conference had proceeded without incident. The next day, however, I received an urgent message from Senator Santorum's office as Joan and I were traveling in Chicago: The Associated Press had just run a story entitled "Likely New Senate Judiciary Chairman Warns Bush Against Nominating Anti-abortion Judges," which *The Washington Post* reprinted. I spoke with Senator Santorum, and he was highly agitated. He urged me to clarify the matter by making a prompt statement that I did not have a litmus test against pro-life judicial nominees. I was glad to do so since this was true, and well supported by my record.

My clarifying statement that day actually reiterated what I had said on numerous prior occasions: "I have supported every one of President Bush's nominees in the Judiciary Committee and on the Senate floor. I have never and would never apply any litmus test on the abortion issue and, as the record shows, I have voted to confirm Chief Justice Rehnquist, Justice O'Connor, and Justice Kennedy and led the fight to confirm Justice Thomas." Indeed, when then-associate justice William H. Rehnquist was nominated for a promotion to chief justice in 1986, his opposition to *Roe* was firmly on record. Moreover, despite the eventual support for upholding *Roe* (in 1992) by Reagan nominees Sandra Day O'Connor and Anthony Kennedy, both were known to have pro-life views when they were nominated, and both issued or joined opinions early in their Supreme Court careers that were highly critical of the abortion-rights cases. My statement also conveyed my concern over "repeated filibusters by the Democrats in the last Senate session" and mentioned my sponsorship of a protocol to set strict time limits that would move nominees along to a prompt vote. I added, "I expect to work well with President Bush in the judicial confirmation process in the years ahead."

Notwithstanding the best efforts of my press office to convey this clarification to interested parties, we were unable to stop the maelstrom. The headlines the next day said it all: "Despite G.O.P. Gain, Fight Over Judges Remains" (*New York Times*); "Specter Denies Warning Bush Over Court Nominees" (*Washington Post*); "Judicial Remarks Stir Conservatives" (*Los Angeles Times*); "Dobson

Blasts Senator Specter's 'Arrogant Grandstanding'; Focus Action Founder Says Republican is Wrong to Threaten Bush Over Nominees" (Associated Press); "Key Senator Denies Warning Bush on Abortion Issue" (Reuters); and "Specter: His Abortion Remark Puts Panel Leadership at Risk" (*Philadelphia Inquirer*). And this was just November 5.

It was all rather ironic when one considers that, three days earlier, I had wrapped up a campaign in which my Democratic opponent had cited my record to charge that a Judiciary Committee under my leadership would push through conservative justices who would reverse key precedents like *Roe*.[2] In the middle of the storm my communications director, Charlie Robbins, told a news producer who was calling him every forty-five minutes, "You're a nice person. I always like to talk to you. But why are you fixated on this?" After all, he noted that Palestinian leader Yasir Arafat was dying; House majority leader Tom DeLay was mired in ethical troubles back home; and war was raging in Sudan. Without missing a beat, the producer replied gleefully, "You're the only scandal in town." Talk about a stressful environment.

To be sure, there were some dissenting voices in the media who recognized what was happening. Brian Wilson of Fox News remarked on the air, "[M]y impression is that Senator Specter was the victim of some spin on the part of some reporters who took some comments and were looking for a . . . good headline out of it." Rush Limbaugh similarly told his radio listeners, "[T]his Specter story . . . may be a story about the media again . . . apparently, just from the looks of this, it may be that some words were put in his mouth that he didn't say." Unfortunately, the media was in such a frenzy that it seemed impervious to my clarifying statement of November 4, so I issued another clarification the next day. This one expanded on the November 4 statement and noted I had "championed the nominations to the Third Circuit" (which handles federal appeals for my home state among other jurisdictions) "of two staunchly conservative pro-life nominees." Once again the effort was futile.

There was some consolation when I traveled that weekend to Miami for a Republican Senatorial Campaign Committee event, where my so-called warning to the president was the talk of the hour. I had a chance to explain the situation to those in attendance, and the audience seemed satisfied. Still, the damage was done among the activists on the right. The politically active religious right readily used—and fed—the media story to wage another campaign, led by Dr. Dobson and his cohorts, to deny me the chairmanship of the Judiciary Committee. That Sunday, Dobson blasted me on the Sunday news show *ABC This Week:*

> Senator Specter is a big-time problem for us, and we're very concerned about him. I campaigned against him. I campaigned on behalf of Toomey, there in Pennsylvania. I thought that the comment that was made by the Senator there . . . was one of the most foolish and ill-considered comments that a politician has made in a long time. President Bush came to Pennsylvania 30-plus times to campaign for him. And the next day after he

wins this mandate, wins this enormous victory, he goes on the air and sticks his thumb in the President's eye. That makes no sense at all. Senator Specter is a problem, not only because of the judiciary but because he has been the champion of stem cell—embryonic stem cell research and so many other things. He's remembered most for having sabotaged Robert Bork. He is a problem, and he must be derailed.

I had a chance to reply later that day on CBS's Sunday talk show, *Face the Nation*. I made the points I had circulated all week and explained that "the concern as to confirmation is really the recognition of a political fact." As President Bush's nominees were being filibustered, I consistently would vote for cloture—to cut off debate so that a vote to confirm the nominee could proceed—but it took sixty votes for cloture, and there were only fifty-five Republicans in the Senate with the last election. "But with 55 Republicans, you aren't at the magic number of 60, so you have to anticipate problems with the Democrats as we have had a lot of them in the past Congress." As for those currently opposing my chairmanship,

these are the same people who came to Pennsylvania from all over the country to try to defeat me in the primary election and they were unsuccessful. They do not like my independence, and I am, I believe, the only pro-choice Republican on the Judiciary Committee, but that doesn't mean that I have a litmus test or that I don't give appropriate deference to whom the president nominates.

Over the next eleven days, I spared no time campaigning to set the record straight—complete with a rigorous schedule of media interviews, meetings with concerned members of the public, and calls to my Senate colleagues. From November 8 through November 18, I was interviewed by twenty-eight different radio, television, and print media outlets, some more than once. My press office was deluged with calls from the media. One day, there were twenty-eight media phone calls to return, which was simply impossible to do with only so many hours in the day and same-day deadlines for reporters. The situation largely resembled a campaign for office, except the voters in this case were Republican members of the Senate.

Some senators had to assign extra personnel to handle the volume of phone calls to their offices. My Judiciary Committee colleague from South Carolina, Lindsey Graham, reworked his office's answering message so that callers would hear, "If you are calling Senator Graham to leave a comment about the Judiciary Committee chairmanship, please press 1. If you would like to be connected to a staff member, please press 2. Senator Graham appreciates you taking the time to call, and have a great day." E-mails to Graham's office alone totaled 15,000.[3] The volume was probably the result of Senator Graham's supportive stance. As he later explained, "Many times Senator Specter is the odd guy out when it comes to policy within the Republican conference. But no one has ever doubted that his disagreements were based on anything other than principle and a sincere look at the issue."

The first call I placed to a Senate colleague in my internal campaign went to Senator Trent Lott of Mississippi. I had spoken out very forcefully on his behalf when the successful effort was made to depose him from the majority leader's position two years earlier. I thought he had been unfairly treated and hoped he would reciprocate. The former majority leader told me he was scheduled to speak to several groups and intimated that he would be helpful. Notwithstanding his words, I ended the call somewhat uneasy at his tone, which seemed equivocal. The conversations that followed produced varying reactions and often transitioned to other issues. Senator Saxby Chambliss of Georgia sounded very supportive, and he volunteered his appreciation for my role in funding the Centers for Disease Control in Atlanta. Senator Sam Brownback of Kansas, a key voice for the religious right, brought up Judge Bork's confirmation with an air of disagreement, but he segued to the Clarence Thomas hearings, noting his appreciation for my role in that nomination. I explained to him the specifics of my recent statement to the press, and he expressed an interest in seeing the transcript, which I was glad to send him. My colleague then brought up legislation he advocated requiring women to be informed of pain to the unborn during certain later-term abortions. I was not familiar with the proposal but replied that, as chairman, I would give fair consideration to any legislative proposals and not use my position to block committee action, even in cases where I might personally oppose the bill. I cited as an example my vote to send Judge Bork to the full Senate even though I had opposed him in committee.

This was an important point for me. I had opposed bottling up nominees and legislation since before my Senate career, when I saw Senator Jim Eastland, the longest-serving chairman of the Judiciary Committee, defeat civil rights legislation during the 1960s by refusing to vote it out of committee to the Senate floor. If the chairman in such cases wants to voice his individual opposition, the place to do it is on the floor, where every senator has a voice. Moving along, I received my most enthusiastic boost from Senator Larry Craig of Idaho, who said he thought I would make a "hell of a Chairman."

My call to Senator Elizabeth Dole of North Carolina was returned by her husband, Bob, who was not sure which Dole I was seeking. He generously volunteered to make a statement on my behalf. Senator John McCain of Arizona, a past and future candidate for president and one of the Senate's most recognizable members, warned me to be cautious of other senators with power interests that might work against me. He followed with a supportive statement on *ABC This Week* the following Sunday: "I've known Arlen for many years. Obviously he is not of the right wing of our party. But I believe that Arlen has done a good job." Senator John Cornyn, himself a former Texas Supreme Court justice and one of the most vocal advocates of the president's judicial nominees, told me my statement had been "blown out of proportion." We should "stand together," he added. Senator Graham, citing a favorite theme, asserted the need to "keep in perspective" the entire matter; he had found me "more than fair." Senator Judd Gregg of New Hampshire flatly told me, "I'll be with you," and became the first senator to make a public statement supporting me. He held a press conference on November 10 in which he spoke kindly of me and added that I was "a tough guy who knows how to run a committee." Senator Pat Roberts of Kansas was another unequivocal supporter, and I appreciated his ability to inject levity into a tense moment. Senator Wayne Allard of Colorado acknowledged that I was misquoted and mistreated. He offered to do what he could to support me but emphasized that he would rather get through the matter without the caucus bringing it to a vote.

Phone calls seemed tentatively to go well with other senators—Craig Thomas of Wyoming, Mel Martinez of Florida, and Kit Bond of Missouri. Senator Hatch, the current chairman, was fully supportive. He rejected concerns that I "was much more liberal than the rest of the members on the committee and that we might not have the leadership we needed to put through judges and other important pieces of legislation." He fully expressed his endorsement to our colleagues—whom he fortunately gauged to be supportive. Senator Hatch's Utah colleague, Bob Bennett, offered one of my earlier public endorsements, calling the dispute a "tempest in a teapot." Most of my colleagues, however, did not initially go public, and

Senator-elect David Vitter of Louisiana expressed "concerns" about my comments.[4] Several if not most sitting Republican senators may have shared the position of Elizabeth Dole, who doubted I would lose the chairmanship but preferred not to inject herself into the controversy.

Additionally, the White House had given me lukewarm support in my fight for the chairmanship. On the first Sunday after the election, the president's senior adviser, Karl Rove, appeared on *Meet the Press* and cited my commitment to "quick hearings, a vote within a reasonable period of time, and that the appellate nominees would be brought to the floor for an up or down vote by the entire Senate." He called me "a man of his word" and added, "We'll take him at his word." To the question of whether President Bush was comfortable with me being chairman, Rove replied, "That's up to the United States Senate to decide, not the president of the United States." Four days later, I attended the White House Veterans Day reception and had a photo op with President Bush. He greeted me warmly and noted that I had been taking quite a lot of heat. I told him that I stood by my commitments of prompt hearings and reporting his nominees from the committee out to the full Senate. He smiled and, in effect, said that was good enough for him. He then commented that Senator Santorum was in for a tough reelection campaign. I told him that reelecting Rick (who was up for reelection in 2006) was my number one priority for the next two years. My relationship with my Senate colleague had been excellent, both professionally and personally, and without his help, I could not have won the primary.

Later on Veterans Day, Roger Stone, a political consultant who had run my campaign for the presidency in the mid-1990s, alarmed me with a report that had traveled via Dr. Dobson: Karl Rove had stated the chairmanship would go to my colleague on the committee, Chuck Grassley of Iowa. Could this possibly be true? Chuck was traveling at the time, but our respective chiefs of staff dispelled the rumor after speaking the next day. Chuck later reminded me that he had earlier committed to support me for the Judiciary Committee as he expected to take the reins of the Finance Committee.

Within the Senate, there did develop a sense among my colleagues, especially some of the "old bulls"—Pete Domenici of New Mexico, Richard Lugar of Indiana, and John Warner of Virginia—that the rules of seniority ought to be respected. Warner, chivalrous as always, told me he "would fall on his sword" to support me, and "the president needed good advice." A crosscurrent swirling throughout the Senate, of course, was the pressure that continued on the part of Dobson and company. Whether that influence was resented or feared (or a little bit of both) was not a question to dwell on. I did not believe the religious right was a monolith, and would not act as if it were. In the middle of my Senate calling spree, I phoned Pat Robertson, whose media empire arguably surpassed Dobson's, and received a sympathetic reaction. On November 10, he remarked on the 700 Club, "I think what is being said about

Senator Specter . . . just is a reflection of a media spin which was relatively inaccurate, and he has certainly clarified over and over again his position."

Like media personalities, senators did not always react predictably. Kay Bailey Hutchison of Texas was pro-choice, but recoiled from the controversy until she ultimately issued a lukewarm endorsement. Fellow committee member Jeff Sessions of Alabama was a question mark for many observers because I had opposed his nomination for a lower federal court judgeship in 1986—a vote I came to regret once I got to know him on the committee. In our conversation over the chairmanship, however, my genial colleague was nothing but supportive about what he called my "great potential to lead the committee."

Amid the whirlwind of controversy, my family experienced a profound loss when our dear friend Paula Kline died on Veterans Day at age fifty-four, following a year and a half battle with breast cancer. Her husband, Tom, had been Shanin's law partner for nearly ten years, but the Specter family had been friends of the Klines for over two decades. A bright, energetic, and spunky lady, Paula was a champion of theater and literature and a devoted mother of two children. I spent the evening she died, then the following afternoon and all day Saturday at the Kline home in Philadelphia. On Sunday morning, November 14, I returned to the political controversy only as long as was required to appear on *ABC This Week*. At 10:00 A.M., I attended Paula's funeral.

Funerals are obviously always sad, but this one was even

more so, because a dreaded disease had cut short Paula's life—a loss that seemed preventable given our ability to fund cancer research. After her casket was lowered into the ground, which is customarily the toughest part of the proceeding, I participated in the Jewish tradition of picking up a shovel and throwing dirt on the coffin. That tradition was followed by Paula's family and closest friends.

The Kline plot was next to the plot that Joan, Shanin, Tracey, and I had purchased a few years earlier in a cemetery located in Bensalem, a suburb of Philadelphia. Tom Kline had sought Shanin's advice on a burial plot when Paula was in extremis, and made a purchase a few yards from our ground. My thoughts went to the inevitable day when my turn would come only a few feet from where we stood. I wondered whether Joan or Shanin or Tracey had similar thoughts, or whether Tom or his daughter Hilary or his son Zac had such thoughts. Hilary, at twenty-five, and Zac, at twenty, probably didn't, but our mortality is never more in mind than when we attend someone else's funeral, especially when our burial place is close at hand.

I thought also of the burial plot of the Kramers and the Fields a short distance away. My close college friend Martin Field had been married to June Kramer, who died tragically in 1971 at the age of thirty-seven from multiple sclerosis. June Kramer Field's death had hit Joan and me particularly hard, because we had been close friends for twenty years. Martin and June and Joan and I had double-dated. After we were married, we later traveled together, with one memorable weekend at Tanglewood in western Massachusetts, where we were introduced to the famous composer-conductor Leonard Bernstein. June was the first of our close-knit group to pass away. It was tough to lose such a close friend at thirty-seven. She was a tall and beautiful brunette. People would frequently comment that she and Joan were the two best lookers in the crowd no matter how many other attractive young women were present. She was the mother of two, Laurel and Stephen, and was a nurturing mother with a creative talent for art.

In the same plot, June's father, Arthur, her mother, Kathryn, and her sister, Lynne, are buried next to her, along with Martin's mother, Hannah Worobe Field. The most beautiful inscription on a cemetery mark that I had ever seen was one composed by Arthur Kramer for his wife, Kathryn: "Step softly. A dream lies buried here."

Washington has a way of rudely interrupting life's most poignant moments. The morning after Paula's funeral, I was back at work and uncertain where I stood with my party. This impression was reinforced when I read of Majority Leader Bill Frist's interview with *Fox News Sunday* the previous day:

> Frist called Specter's comments "disheartening" and was noncommittal on whether he would support him as chairman. As for whether Specter had made a persuasive case to head the panel, Frist said, "Not yet. But I've talked to Arlen, and he is talking to lots of different people now."[5]

The majority leader also stated that "whoever that Chairman is" should "have a strong predisposition" to support President Bush's nominees "with adequate debate and discussion," to take nominees "all the way to the floor and to have a strong predisposition of supporting that candidate, including on the floor of the United States Senate." I spoke that Monday evening to Senator Frist, and he spoke in such supportive terms that it was hard to believe he was the same person who made those comments on television the day before. The majority leader outlined a process in which I would meet with Republican members, and we would seek an affirmative statement from the Judiciary Committee. We would try to bring the matter to closure by the end of the week.

Amid another week of calls to senators, I met with Republican leadership that Tuesday, November 16, in the majority leader's office in the Capitol. The senators who were present spoke for about a half hour before inviting me in to our first meeting of the day, at 11:00 A.M. The meeting was primarily about process. Senator Frist spoke about his desire to bring closure, and the other senators present who spoke—McCain, Bennett, Gregg, and Jon Kyl of Arizona, a fellow committee member—seemed supportive of me. I walked out of the office with Senator Frist to find an enormous gaggle of press. If *The Washington Post* was correct, ours appeared to be the most interesting Senate story of the day. It was attended by about fifty reporters. Another twenty followed Senator Harry Reid of Nevada, who had just been

elected the new Democratic leader, and four more trailed
Senator Kerry to record the rare occurrence of a losing
presidential candidate returning to the Senate. Meanwhile,
what were reported to be several pro-life, church-based
groups launched a demonstration they called a pray-in outside the Dirksen Senate Office Building, where the Judiciary Committee hearing room is housed. The evening
news would broadcast Reverend Patrick J. Mahoney, director of the Christian Defense Coalition, calling out, "Senator
Specter must not assume that position!"[6]

Another meeting in the leader's office followed at four
that afternoon with Republican members of the Judiciary
Committee. Again, the comments I heard were very supportive. The closest the meeting came to debate was over
the question of whether I ought to put something in writing as an assurance to my colleagues. Senator Craig was
emphatically in favor of a written statement, which members could then show their constituents. Senator Chambliss discouraged the idea. I remarked that I was glad to put
something in writing. I thought it better to have a written
statement, so my commitments could be limited to what
was in writing and no one would be able to hold me to an
alleged oral promise I never made. During a light breakfast and long meeting of the Republican Conference the
next morning, I tried to scratch out a written statement.
Most of that meeting was dedicated to conference business, including votes on officers and rules, but Senator
Hatch and I each had a chance afterward to make a case
for my chairmanship. We kept it short, because it had

been a long morning and people were not in much of a mood to listen.

There was still an air of uncertainty that day when Senator Lamar Alexander of Tennessee told CNN "it sounded like" I "was issuing a warning to the president about the kind of nominations he ought to send. . . . It sounded like Senator Specter might have a litmus test, and I don't think the Judiciary Committee ought to have a litmus test." When Alexander solicited my vote against Lott two years later for assistant minority leader, I was tempted to ask him about those comments, but didn't. I would cast the deciding vote for Lott, who narrowly carried the Republican members by a vote of 25 to 24, but I left 2004 out of the equation. I was more concerned about who could do the most to assist the party. Alexander would have less time for the job because he was in cycle for reelection, and Lott was more experienced.

By that Thursday, November 18, 2004, I had my statement fairly well outlined and reviewed it with several members of the committee. It was largely a rehash of my repeated statements about not employing a litmus test to deny confirmation for nominees or bottling up legislation I opposed in committee. I excluded the provision Senator Frist had mentioned on the previous Sunday's television program about expecting the chairman "to have a strong predisposition" to support President Bush's nominees and substituted a considerably milder sentence drafted by Shanin: "I have no reason to believe that I'll be unable to support any individual President Bush finds worthy of nomination." I was not entirely happy with that sentence, but agreed to it given the lack of a better alternative. Besides, I always have had great confidence in Shanin's judgment. Regarding the filibuster, my statement noted:

> I have already registered my opposition to the Democrats' filibusters with 17 floor statements and will use my best efforts to stop any future filibusters. It is my hope and expectation that we can avoid future filibusters and judicial gridlock with a 55–45 Republican majority and election results demonstrating voter dissatisfaction with Democratic filibusters. If a rule change is necessary to avoid filibusters, there are relevant recent precedents to secure rule changes with 51 votes.[7]

Senator Hatch convened the Republican members of the committee that afternoon, where some final modifications were made to the statement before the members— all but Senator Grassley, who was busy with daylong hearings—appeared at 3:15 P.M. for a press conference in the Senate Radio/TV Gallery in the Capitol. Senator Hatch opened as follows:

> I'm pleased to announce that the Judiciary Committee has had a number of meetings, and although this decision has to be made after January 4th, I'm pleased to announce that there is unanimity among all current members of the committee, all of whom I believe will be on the committee after the 1st of the year, that Arlen

Specter will be our next Chairman of the Senate Judiciary Committee. And we are pleased to support Arlen in this matter. He is senior. He has done an excellent job in supporting the president over the last number of years that I've been Chairman. He's been a tremendous asset to me through my tenure as Chairman. And I have nothing but the highest respect for Arlen Specter.

The ordeal was finally over. It remained to be formalized in early January, but the grueling effort and suspense surrounding the chairmanship were finally gone. Still, the last fifteen days had been a torturous journey that basically ended where it began. During the press conference of November 18, an interesting exchange occurred between a reporter and Senator Hatch:

Question: Could you explain what's different today than two weeks ago when this first started? What have you heard from Senator Specter yesterday and the day before that some of you didn't already know who have worked with him on the committee for eight years?

Senator Hatch: Let me take a crack at that. You know, I said to Arlen after this broke that Arlen certainly has an ability to get media attention, jokingly. Because let me tell you, this is a tough position, and virtually everything you say as Chairman of the committee and as a member of the committee is going to be criticized and sometimes distorted and sometimes misconstrued, sometimes highly criticized. And this is just something, you know, that we had to work through, because—I can't speak for Arlen, but I can say that he didn't mean it the way some in the media interpreted it. So we've resolved these problems. We're unanimous in support of Arlen Specter, as we should be. Our caucus is a broad, diverse caucus. And frankly, we love everybody in the Republican caucus.[8]

Shortly before this exchange, I remarked to a reporter, "If I do not act with independence, it will be the first time in my life."

The outcomes of the Toomey primary and the chairmanship dispute may have been healthy for the party, if not for my own personal health. Particularly in the two-party system we have in this country, a party that succumbs to doctrinal rigidity and closes its big tent runs the risk of marginalizing itself and, more important, intensifying the ideological polarization that increasingly has characterized our politics. For these reasons, the defeat of Senator Lieberman, a moderate Democrat, in Connecticut's Democratic primary in 2006 struck me as an unhealthy development both for that party and for the system. On our end, the Republican membership of the Judiciary Committee arguably showed even greater ideological diversity after the committee was reorganized than before. Senators Craig and Chambliss left the committee after 2004, and two of the most conservative members of the Senate would join us: Sam Brownback and Senator-elect Tom Coburn of Oklahoma. A comment was made to me that both members would be difficult to handle on the committee, but upon hearing their preferences to serve on the committee, I called each of them to extend my welcome. I reiterated to Senator Brownback that whether or not I agreed with legislation he was interested in passing, I would vote it out of committee, reserving the right to object to it on the floor. As chairman, I knew that I had to keep every Republican member of the committee on my side, and, in any event, it better served the institution not to have major legislation die in committee. In our dealings, I would be careful not to be patronizing, but to make realistic accommodations consistent with my views on the substance of the issues, and also with a broader view as to what the chairman should do in trying to accommodate members.

In retrospect, I believe the campaign against my chairmanship likely would have occurred in some form even absent my postelection remarks. The far right had been in high gear and ready to do battle from the moment the presidential election was behind them. By speaking as I did, however, I had given the opposition an opening. My father had the following admonition: "Know what you say; don't say what you know." Looking back at my postelection press conference, I should have been more guarded in my language—notwithstanding the accuracy of the observation that the president would have a hard time getting pro-life judges confirmed. I pride myself on speaking candidly, but in politics words can be construed the wrong way as well as the right way.

Looking back on 2004, Shanin perceptively noted that I

faced not two, but virtually three elections that year. In all three, I stuck to my guns and my principles. Whatever the cause-and-effect relationship between my experiences that year and my health, I began to feel immense fatigue after the general election. Between November and December, I visited doctors in Philadelphia and Washington with that complaint. I saw the Senate doctor as early as November 15 for fatigue and again on the twenty-ninth for what the doctor recorded as "fatigue and malaise." On November 26, I was so exhausted that I recorded in my small black datebook calendar, the closest thing I keep to a diary, that I "felt drugged almost." Not that I was any more inclined to take myself away from work. After a November 30 dinner at the Prime Rib, one of my favorite Washington restaurants, Carl Feldbaum told me, "You're seventy-four. You drive yourself like you're twenty-four. Why don't you take two hours off?"

I replied, "I just did!"

Still, I found myself making frequent trips to my "hide-away"—a cozy office in the Capitol two minutes off the Senate floor that I had by virtue of seniority—to take afternoon naps. I certainly did not want to think the issue was age, yet David Brog, who had worked for me for over six years since the mid-1990s, never saw me so "wiped out." Perhaps a rough year had just taken its toll. Shanin thought I was experiencing a postelection letdown, which even he had encountered when the sustained frenetic activity of a campaign ended. Maybe the problem was related to a hernia which was operated on at Jefferson

Hospital in Philadelphia on December 10. It might have explained the fatigue. At least that seemed plausible to my doctors and me when I canceled a planned trip to Iraq in mid-December. During a December 29 lunch with Carolyn Short, a prominent Philadelphia attorney I was trying to bring to my staff, my prospective employee noticed the fatigue and even a trace of sweat. The campaign must have taken a lot out of me, she said. No, I responded, I was just suffering from a virus. I was sure of it. As I looked forward to 2005, the only new challenge I envisioned was the chairmanship.

3

An Unwanted Birthday Present

I T HAD BEEN a long journey to the chairmanship. In a broad sense, my preparation for the job dated back to my participation in my high school and college debating teams, which taught the skills of analysis and extemporaneous speaking. I have a reputation for being prosecutorial, but that trait really is a reflection of an analytical tendency to pursue all the facts, which inevitably entails probing for answers. Those happen to be natural traits for a career in law, whether as a prosecutor, a Warren Commission staffer, or a Judiciary Committee member. My legal background made that committee my keenest interest as I pursued my first Senate committee assignments back in 1981. Even then, however, there were portents of what was to come. The chairman at the time, Strom Thurmond of South Carolina, did his best to keep me off the committee because I was not conservative. He created two subcommittees as inducements to two new members to join and unsuccessfully solicited several other senators, but there was still a spot open when my turn came.[1]

My early time in the Senate was a great learning experience in itself, with no shortage of colleagues who taught by example how business should be conducted. Howard Baker was the majority leader when I joined the Senate, and to this day I consider him a cut above the rest. He was a brilliant man who ran the chamber with an iron hand[2] and managed to amass tremendous legislative victories while maintaining civility across party lines. If my generation had a Great Compromiser in the mold of Henry Clay, Daniel Webster, and John C. Calhoun, he was it. I also admired Henry "Scoop" Jackson of Washington and was privileged to get the opportunity to know him during my early years in the Senate before he died in September 1983. A centrist in his own party, he was affable and approachable to his colleagues and a tireless worker on behalf of his constituents. Bob Dole was another exemplar of Senate leadership. Whether the Republicans were in the majority or the minority, he had a knack for working well with colleagues without leaving his wit and humor behind. I also hold Joe Biden of Delaware in high esteem. He chaired the Judiciary Committee from 1987 to 1995 and left an example of fairness and efficiency in how to run a committee—not to mention a knack for keeping committee business interesting to observers. Joe still serves on the Judiciary Committee, and our many train rides together enabled us to become good friends. His future would include service as chairman of the Foreign Relations Committee and an attempt at his party's nomination for president in 2008.

The Judiciary Committee has one of the broadest jurisdictions in the Senate. It takes up issues ranging from criminal justice to antitrust and intellectual property law, including such sensitive issues as the Constitution, civil rights, and the composition of the federal courts. The committee is responsible for most matters governing the federal judiciary and the Department of Justice, the principal law enforcement arm of the federal government. This includes confirmation of the president's nominees to serve as judges on the federal bench or as principal officers of the Justice Department.

While nominations come from the president, bills are typically introduced by senators or arrive after being passed by the House. After a bill or a nominee within the committee's jurisdiction is referred to it, the committee deliberates on the issue in a process that typically includes holding hearings to gather relevant information. The next level of review consists of executive business meetings, also called markup sessions, during which revisions to legislation are made or nominees considered by committee members. If a majority of the committee votes its approval, the bill or the nomination is reported out to the full Senate, where it is placed on the calendar for the entire body to consider. At that stage, debate before the full Senate usually occurs before the matter—including any amendments, in the case of legislation—is submitted to a vote on the floor before the entire body. A nomination is confirmed once the Senate votes its approval, but legislation requires House passage and then approval of a House-Senate conference committee before going to the president for his signature or veto.

The Judiciary Committee of the 109th Congress in 2005 provided an interesting mix of liberal and conservative, with members like Ted Kennedy and Democratic whip Richard Durbin on the left and Jon Kyl and John Cornyn on the right—now to be joined by Sam Brownback and Tom Coburn. Perhaps by virtue of its vast authority, the committee has long been one of the most politically charged places on Capitol Hill. In an era when politics is more polarized than usual, that makes for a potentially explosive situation. Committee chairmen in the Senate, who always come from the majority party, share certain leadership functions with the ranking minority member—a role performed by Pat Leahy between the Republicans' recapture of the Senate in 2003, when he gave up the gavel, and the Democrats' return in 2007, when he regained it.

Senator Leahy has the distinction of being the only Democrat ever elected to the Senate by the State of Vermont[3]—a state that was once so Republican, it voted against Franklin D. Roosevelt all four times he ran for president. Pat reflected his state's ideological transition over the last generation and had gained prominence during his thirty years in the Senate. We first met at the 1969 summer conference of the National District Attorneys Association in Philadelphia, which I hosted while I was district attorney and he was the state's attorney for Chittenden County, Vermont. By 2005, Pat had the grandfatherly bearing of an elder statesmen—I say this fully aware he is ten years my junior—but he was always ready for combat. We did not interact extensively in the Senate before 2005, but that was about to change.

Before the chairman's gavel was in my hand, I called my colleague and walked over to his office—over his protest, as he felt he should come to my office. Unfortunately, Pat's relationship with the outgoing chairman, Orrin Hatch, had been awful, and I wanted to set the right pace for our working relationship. In our discussion, Pat was as gracious to me as one could imagine. "Arlen, you're made to be chairman," he intoned, joking that I was one of the two people he would most like to see as chairman—the other inferentially being himself. We agreed that the committee had become polarized, almost to the extent that it was nonfunctioning, and Pat remarked that he felt we could work well together. I assured him that he would get no surprises from me. Advance consultation with him would be a priority.

Twenty-four years had passed for me in the Senate when my term as chairman of the Judiciary Committee officially began on Tuesday, January 4, 2005, the start of the new session of Congress. I was sworn in that day for my fifth term, with family and friends joining me to mark the occasion. Outwardly, I appeared to be in good health, but for a bandage on the bridge of my nose that covered a skin lesion I had had treated four weeks earlier. I even felt a respite from my fatigue. During the lunchtime reception following my swearing-in ceremony, there was a certain sense of relief that bordered on exuberance. My granddaughter Perri, now out of campaign mode, took the microphone at one point to inform the crowd, "You don't have to vote for Arlen anymore," to which I replied, "Or any less." The rest of the day was dominated by the business of organizing the 109th Congress.

As the new Congress began, the committee would have a full agenda, including the confirmation of a new attorney general, Alberto Gonzales, and legislation on class-action lawsuits, bankruptcy reform, and asbestos litigation reform. Asbestos reform promised to be the most complex undertaking. The class-action bill sought to reduce frivolous class-action lawsuits and the practice known as forum shopping, in which lawyers attempt to file lawsuits in favorable jurisdictions. The bankruptcy reform bill sought to curb the widespread abuse of the bankruptcy laws so that they would serve their intended purpose of financial protection for vulnerable consumers rather than being manipulated as a tool of financial planning. This work occupied most of my schedule for the first two months of the new year.

I made the confirmation of Gonzales, a former Texas Supreme Court justice then serving as White House counsel, the committee's top priority. I scheduled his nomination hearing for Thursday, January 6, two days after the new senators were sworn in. That hearing marked the first public meeting of the reconstituted eighteen-member

Judiciary Committee of the 109th Congress, and it was there that I would formally take the gavel. Since considerable media attention was expected, I suggested to Senator Leahy that we walk into the hearing room together for the cameras with Gonzales, which Pat appreciated. Shortly after convening the hearing, I paid tribute to outgoing chairman Hatch for handling "these duties in an atmosphere sometimes contentious, sometimes difficult, but always with good cheer and always with aplomb and always with balance." I also referred to the nickname I gave him, "Iron Pants," a wry tribute to his stamina through committee business regardless of how tedious and protracted it became. Orrin responded very kindly and handed me the gavel with a wide grin just before Senator Leahy patted my shoulder.

The Gonzales hearing was largely about the conduct of the war on terror, but it also included the standard Justice Department issues of immigration, antitrust laws, intellectual property rights, and organized and violent crime. Back in 2000, I wrote in my autobiography that "nuclear, biological, and chemical weapons of mass destruction pose the single greatest threat to the United States and the world" and that "[a]s we begin the twenty-first century, terrorism has replaced classic warfare as the means of achieving political objectives."[4] The nation began to focus on these issues after the September 11 terrorist attacks the following year. During the Gonzales hearings, I cited "the threat of terrorism" as "the most important issue facing the country," including "how we deal with it in the balance of our civil rights." Both protesters and supporters of the Bush administration were visible in the back of the hearing room as questions and answers on both sides explored the treatment of captured detainees and how to go about reauthorizing the soon-to-expire Patriot Act as a tool in fighting the war on terror.

Gonzales was closely questioned, really treated pretty roughly, by Leahy and especially Kennedy. The nominee was widely blamed by Democrats for a Justice Department memo from an assistant attorney general named Jay Bybee that was addressed to him as White House counsel and ran well below the mark in defining how far the interrogation of terrorist suspects could go without violating the rules on torture. Although he was the recipient of the memo, the attack smacked of guilt by association, as neither he nor his office had prepared the memo. "[T]he Bybee torture memoranda, written at your request . . . made abuse of interrogation easier," thundered Kennedy in the hearing room before he asked his first question.

The Massachusetts senator pressed for multiple rounds of questioning, and I accommodated him with extra rounds, but I limited them to ten minutes each. It was my thinking that he would have a harder time asking for a fifth round than he would for a third or fourth, even if the earlier rounds were elongated to twenty or more minutes. I knew it was indispensable to treat Gonzales's opponents fairly, but to be fair to Gonzales at the same time, he could not be hung out to dry indefinitely, and my goal was to get him off the witness stand by the end of the day. Hearings

ˉfrequently start with a bang and a sizzle and then peter out after lunch as the afternoon drags out. This one was no exception, and I was able to get Gonzales off the stand by 4:30, which, some commented, was an accomplishment. When John Bolton's confirmation to be ambassador to the United Nations was rejected in the following year, the comment was frequently made that had he been on and off the hearing table in a day, he would have been confirmed.

By ending at 4:30, I was able to get the second and final panel of outside witnesses on in the late afternoon without according Gonzales's critics prime time the following morning. I was tempted to keep those second panel witnesses on longer because they were very distinguished: John Hutson, president and dean of the Franklin Pierce Law Center; Douglas Johnson, executive director of the Center for Victims of Torture; and Harold Hongju Koh, dean of the Yale Law School. Their focus was on torture. I had read the comments of some experts who defended torture in the so-called ticking bomb cases, and in a sense would have been interested to hear their testimony at some length. However, since Gonzales had not written the interrogation memo, rendering the issue peripheral to his confirmation, I wanted to move ahead to complete the hearings so that the committee could turn its attention to the list of other very important subjects. When I later thought about how tension might have caused or exacerbated my medical condition, my mind went back to the Gonzales hearing, where we had some tense moments.

Giving the nominee's Democratic opponents full sway in the hearing process while finishing expeditiously required repeated colloquies with Kennedy before my colleague relented.

Involved as the Gonzales nomination was, I spent nearly every day of my first week as chairman working on the issue of asbestos litigation reform, a controversial issue arising from a long history of litigation by workers injured by exposure to asbestos. I first learned of the problem in 1983 when Senator Gary Hart of Colorado sought my help. His key constituent among Colorado corporations, the construction material producer Johns Manville, was nearing bankruptcy because of the asbestos claims it faced. The problem defied solution for two decades until Chairman Hatch introduced legislation in 2003 providing for a $140 billion trust fund that would pay claims on a no-fault basis without going to court. With over seventy companies facing bankruptcy, thousands of workers suffering from mesothelioma, a form of cancer generally caused by exposure to asbestos, would not be compensated unless something was done.

During the Senate's August 2003 recess, at my request, Judge Edward R. Becker of the Third Circuit brought the so-called asbestos stakeholders (manufacturers, insurers, labor representatives, and trial lawyers) into his Philadelphia chambers to mediate their disagreements in the first of more than fifty knock-down, drag-out negotiating sessions. The first sessions lasted two days. Most subsequent meetings occurred in the conference room of my Washington Senate office, with Ed sitting next to me at the head of a long table. The qualities that earned him tremendous respect—as a jurist and as a man—made him a great ally in attempting to hammer out the best possible solution to the asbestos litigation problem. Ed was a brilliant, warm, outgoing, caring, supremely friendly individual whom people liked instantly. He always remembered names and took the time to learn about the families and interests of those he encountered. The effect of such attentiveness to colleagues who are undertaking an arduous endeavor is not to be underestimated.

With over twenty stakeholders on four opposing sides in the typically tense meeting atmosphere, Ed knew how to break the ice: How is your new baby doing? Are you getting enough sleep? Others would chime in with their comparable experiences. He possessed less ego than anyone I have ever met, but he was so accomplished that he was selected from the 862 sitting federal judges to receive the coveted Edward J. Devitt Distinguished Service to Justice Award in 2002. He was far more easygoing than I. He was the epitome of patience, while I was almost his counterpart of impatience. He presided over our asbestos meetings knowing that effective negotiation would require everyone to have an opportunity to speak. I typically left it up to him to conduct the meetings and became more involved when I thought it necessary to pick up the pace. He worked on the asbestos legislation for the next thirty-four months, while maintaining a full load as a circuit judge at the same time as he was suffering from an advanced stage of prostate cancer.

I had known Ed for over fifty years and considered him one of my best friends. I first met him in the fall of 1950 when we rode the Frankford elevated train together each morning from our homes in Northeast Philadelphia to the University of Pennsylvania. At Penn, we were on the debating team. One highly publicized contest took place against the Norfolk, Massachusetts, Model State Prison team in 1952, before approximately eight hundred inmates—truly a captive audience. The prison team took the affirmative on the subject: Resolved that the Communist Party should be outlawed. Editors from the then-five Boston newspapers voted four to one that the prisoners won the debate.

I was three years Ed's senior in college, but due to my Air Force service, I was just a year ahead of him when we both attended Yale Law School. Our wives were classmates as well: Joan Levy, later Specter, sat next to Flora Lyman, later Becker, in alphabetical order in Olney High School. After graduation, we kept in touch as we pursued our respective legal and political careers. Ed was active in Republican politics well before my introduction to the Republican Party in my first election bid, and he provided invaluable representation when my eligibility to run for mayor was challenged three times before the Supreme Court of Pennsylvania in 1967. With his assistance, we won all three cases. Had I followed his political advice as well as his legal advice, I probably would have been elected mayor. But who knows how my future path would have changed?

A lawyer's lawyer and a judge's judge, Ed had sat on the federal bench since 1970. In May 2003, he stepped down as chief judge of the Third Circuit at age seventy to assume senior status, which ordinarily entails significantly reduced judicial duties, but not for him. He was then fighting a grueling battle with prostate cancer, but his illness did not deter him from taking on the asbestos issue that summer. The 108th Congress would end without resolution, giving us a goal during the 109th Congress and setting the stage for a number of hearings. The day after I became chairman, Ed helped me prepare for the first of these hearings, which occurred on January 11.

The hearings did not occur a day too soon. The fatigue that had hit me the previous months intensified, and I left with Joan for Palm Springs, Florida, on January 12 in the hope that I would feel better in the warm climate. Normally, I like to play squash and work when I travel, but this time, I had no inclination to do so. A mere mile-and-a-quarter walk back to our hotel from a casual trip to a shoe store turned out to be grueling. I spent most of my time in Florida in bed or listlessly soaking up sunshine. I still did not feel better, so after returning, I went for the first of three weekly acupuncture treatments in Bethesda, Maryland, at the recommendation of Joan and several friends. I had read some encouraging literature on the procedure and found it helpful in alleviating a shoulder problem during the late 1980s, but this time the acupuncture provided no relief.

Several days after returning from Florida, I chaired a contentious committee markup session on Judge Gonzales, followed by President Bush's second inauguration the next day. Chief Justice William Rehnquist, who had been missing sessions of the Supreme Court while fighting thyroid cancer, arrived just long enough to administer the oath. He walked slowly with the aid of a cane and kept a scarf wrapped around his throat. He had performed this duty at every inauguration since that of President Bush's father, but following a tracheotomy, his powerful baritone voice had given way to a high-pitched intonation that was jarring to those who knew him. Whatever was in store for the Court in the near future, it was simultaneously poignant and inspiring to witness the chief justice rise to the challenge of what would be his last inauguration. I was impressed and gratified to see him there, answering the call of duty.

During the following week, on Wednesday, January 26, the committee had to continue with the Gonzales nomination, since we had not reached a vote the prior week, and it finally reported him out to the floor in a party-line vote. Every committee Democrat voted against the nomination while every Republican voted in favor of it, a scenario that had become all too familiar. I had hoped to see Judge Gonzales get more bipartisan support. The floor debate was lively, and what should not have been a contentious nomination—his predecessor, John Ashcroft, had been considered more controversial—would end ultimately with

Gonzales being confirmed by the full Senate by a vote of 60 to 36. He carried fewer minority-party votes than any nominee for attorney general in 80 years.[5]

I was so exhausted the weekend after the final Gonzales markup that I slept for thirteen hours that Saturday—a personal record. I had my last acupuncture appointment the following Monday and looked forward to the president's State of the Union address two days later. As the traditional response to the Constitution's mandate that the president "shall from time to time give to the Congress Information of the State of the Union," this speech has become a significant annual event in which members of both the Senate and the House crowd into the House chamber to hear the president. Everyone is on his or her best behavior, if for no other reason than the roving TV camera, which might catch you at any moment. At my first such event, in 1981, Senator Paul Laxalt warned me not to doze off. Senator Sam Hayakawa had done so the year before, and was embarrassed on national TV.[6]

After a busy day that included another committee hearing on the issue of asbestos, I walked outside the Russell Rotunda, part of the Senate's oldest office building, to be interviewed at 6:30 P.M. by CNN host Lou Dobbs. It took the production crew what seemed like an eternity to prepare, and I found it so difficult to withstand the chilly air that I retreated inside, only to go outside when I felt I could again test my endurance. I repeated my treks inside and outside several times before the interview was ready to start, and thankfully the interview itself went smoothly. I then went over to the Senate dining room in the Capitol for dinner with Carolyn Short, the recently arrived general counsel for the Judiciary Committee. As we tried to discuss business, I was overcome by an awful feeling of exhaustion and feverishness. Carolyn, who had noticed my fatigue and perspiration during our December 29 lunch, was alarmed, she told me later, to see beads of perspiration on the back of my neck. She asked what was wrong, and I replied, "I just can't seem to kick this virus." By the end of dinner, I had had enough. I went home early and missed the State of the Union address for the first time in my twenty-four years in the Senate. I arose the following morning in time for a 7:30 A.M. interview on C-SPAN's *Washington Journal* regarding the Gonzales floor vote that day, but my body told me I had to see a doctor. I was surprised when a *Washington Post* reporter later called me to inquire as to why I had missed the president's speech. The media rarely missed something if it made you look bad.

I went with Joan, Shanin, Tracey, and their oldest daughter, Silvi, to the Super Bowl in Jacksonville, Florida, the following Sunday. It was the first time the Eagles had been in the Super Bowl since 1981 and only the second time in the history of the event. I was a rabid Eagles fan going back to the 1950s, when Chuck Bednarik used to tackle Jimmy Brown in Franklin Field. The trip had been planned for some time, and the day turned out to be long and tiring. We flew down in the morning, had lunch, and attended several Super Bowl parties before the game itself. My malaise extended well beyond the Philadelphia Eagles losing to the New England Patriots by a score of 24 to 21, which was closer than the game itself. It was a long walk back to our car, but that was the fastest exit because of the large crowd. We flew back after the game, arriving in Philadelphia after two in the morning, but in time to make my Monday doctor's appointment. I went to see my Philadelphia doctors the next day, February 7, but they seemed to have little idea of what was wrong with me. One of them, Dr. David Capuzzi, mentioned only a blood test showing an irregular level of "C-reactive protein," an indicator of an inflammation in the body, but he did not consider it medically definitive.

I had a week ahead of me that was divided among the issues of class-action lawsuit reform, asbestos, and bankruptcy reform. That Thursday I made it over to Dr. John Eisold, the Capitol's attending physician, after chairing a bankruptcy reform hearing. Noting my continued elevated temperature, my fatigue, and the blood-test results, the doctor expressed the opinion that I might have an unusual virus or perhaps a "malignancy." That word sounded an alarm. It kept ringing in my ears after I heard it, but I still had two votes to cast on the Senate floor and a meeting to organize the Appropriations Committee before the day's Senate work was finished. One of the votes was for the class-action bill, the Class Action Fairness Act, which passed the Senate and went on to become one of the first laws to come out of the 109th Congress. After my D.C. work was finished for the day, I returned to Philadelphia, where my primary care physician, Dr. Geno Merli, conducted a CT scan among other tests on Friday at Jefferson Hospital. I left there without any definitive word on what was wrong, and would have to return Monday for a biopsy.

The day after my hospital visit, February 12, was my seventy-fifth birthday. A lot of time seemed to have passed since my last birthday, when I attended a Harrisburg campaign event with the president during my primary. I had decided to skip the birthday celebration because I was not pleased about turning seventy-five and did not want to think about my advancing age. As it turned out, Mother Nature took care of the celebration for me. I awoke that morning with a fever and chills. Since I was not up to the fifteen-minute drive to Shanin's house, he and Tracey brought Silvi and their other daughters—Perri, Lilli, and Hatti—to see me at my house in Philadelphia. Ages four through eleven at the time, my grandchildren are a delight to see, but I'm afraid I was not much fun that day. I spent most of their visit talking with them in my living room chair in something of a haze. Silvi worried that something was wrong. Although I was not quite bedridden, I thought the visit bore some resemblance to an old movie deathbed scene, but I kept that to myself.

With the intimation of "malignancy" on my mind, I decided to call Dr. John Glick for consultation that afternoon. He asked why I called him, and I replied, "I saw your name written in the sky." That was shorthand for his extraordinary reputation as one of America's preeminent oncologists. In fact, I had been recommended to another

physician at Jefferson who was described to me as a protégé of Dr. Glick, but I thought, "Why settle for the protégé
when the mentor is within reach?" While there are lots of
deterrents to a career in elective politics, an underestimated benefit is the access to better health care. I had
known Dr. Glick in passing for over a decade. He was a political supporter who shared much of his profession's interest in the NIH and other public health initiatives I
promoted on the Appropriations Committee. A scholarly
man and the consummate professional, I would learn as I
became his patient just how bright, capable, and dedicated to his patients he was. Since my Jefferson Hospital
visit the previous day had prompted press inquiries, Dr.
Glick graciously made a house call the following afternoon to accommodate my concern about privacy.

My birthday illness was still with me the next day. Sitting in my sun room, I was pale and had a temperature,
and I was wrapped in a blanket to overcome the chills.
Joan and Shanin were with me, and when the doctor arrived, he immediately took charge in a three-hour session
that impressed me with his thoroughness. Despite my
condition, I was alert and anxious to learn what was wrong
with me. I gave him a detailed history of my condition, including my months-long fatigue since the election and
my more recent fevers, which were as high as 102 de-
grees. I experienced no weight loss or itching, but the
doctor noticed a symptom that I—and the other doctors
who had checked me the last several months—had not:
swollen lymph glands. Joan and Shanin would express

considerable irritation over this failure on the part of previous doctors. Dr. Glick conducted a thorough physical examination in my bedroom, where he checked lymph nodes under my arms, in my neck, and elsewhere in my body. He also examined my lungs, liver, and spleen. After the examination, we returned to the sun room, where I asked Dr. Glick, "What do you think's going on?" He responded that he thought it very likely the combination of swollen glands, fever, fatigue, and chills indicated that I had either Hodgkin's disease or non-Hodgkin's lymphoma.

Non-Hodgkin's lymphoma is a term that refers to a collection of twenty or more different kinds of cancer of the lymphatic system. They can occupy a wide range from low to high grade, with a corresponding range of survivability. Hodgkin's disease is a common form of lymphoma that can be distinguished under a microscope by the presence of giant cells known as Reed-Sternberg cells. Whether a patient is afflicted with either disease can be detected only by conducting a biopsy to analyze body tissue, and Dr. Glick arranged for my biopsy at Jefferson Hospital the next day to include a lymph node above my left collarbone as well as a bone marrow biopsy. I underwent surgery to remove the lymph nodes as scheduled and spent a rough night at the hospital, waking up at 3:00 A.M., unable to sleep further. I was released by midmorning with no word on the results, which were still being studied.

I felt lousy when I returned home that Tuesday afternoon, but I was determined to keep up my work schedule as best I could. I had a long meeting in the early afternoon with my chief counsel, Michael O'Neill, chief of staff David Brog, and Peter Jensen, who supervised nominations, to discuss judicial nominees coming up for confirmation. Dr. Glick interrupted that call with another three-hour house visit where he relayed to me—"pending further studies"— the tentative test results: The lymph node biopsy showed Hodgkin's disease. Although my bone marrow tested negative by CT scan, both sides of my diaphragm showed enlarged lymph nodes indicating Stage IIIB Hodgkin's disease. The pertinent scale range is I to IV, with IV being the most advanced stage. My fever and sweats indicated what oncologists refer to as B symptoms of the disease, which indicate a more severe condition. Although Hodgkin's is a disease of unknown cause, it is one of the most curable known forms of cancer. "Since it's curable," I thought, "let's get to it."

"Tell me what I need to do to be cured," I asked the doctor. The first thing Dr. Glick explained he would attempt to do was alleviate my exhaustion, fever, and the sweating, but fortunately, my diagnosis allowed us to aim for cure as our ultimate goal. Treatment would consist of chemotherapy, which would be administered every two weeks for a total of twelve to sixteen treatments over twenty-four to thirty-two weeks, depending on my response. Hopefully, Dr. Glick continued, we could keep it at twelve, because he knew how eager I was to devote myself to my work. PET (Positron Emission Tomography) and CT (Computerized Tomography) scans would track my response, and if the disease completely disappeared—clinically referred to as a complete response, or complete remission—the treatments would stop at twelve.

I asked how I would tolerate chemotherapy. The procedure was, after all, known to incur a host of side effects. Precisely how many I did not know until Dr. Glick laid them out for me. He explained that he would administer strong antinausea medications just prior to the chemotherapy, which was known to cause nausea and vomiting. My fatigue would diminish initially as treatment began, but as it progressed, chemotherapy would cause more fatigue. I would probably develop an anemia, which would require additional drugs in response. My white blood cell count would diminish, creating the risk of infection. Other possible side effects included mouth and tongue sores, numbness in the fingers and toes, and redness of the skin and certain areas of the joints. There were also rare possibilities of developing lung or heart toxicities, getting a second tumor, and a 1 to 2 percent chance of dying from complications with chemotherapy. The latter figure may seem remote, but those were the very complications that took Paula Kline's life. Finally, there was a better than 90 percent chance I would lose my hair. If I experienced any signs of infection or a temperature above 100.5, I was to call Dr. Glick immediately. That said, the doctor explained that there were a tremendous number of medicines available to combat the side effects of chemotherapy, and he gave me several prescriptions. That, plus a positive mental attitude, would go a long way. Some side effects, such as mouth sores, could not be prevented, but they could be treated. The hair loss was guaranteed to be temporary. The hair follicles would remain in place, so my hair likely would return fuller and in its natural color.

He added that although I was seventy-five years old, my body physiology was considerably younger. My heart, liver, and kidneys were functioning well, though he wanted to run a series of tests the next day. He underscored that he had advocated since the 1970s that chronological age is not a barrier to cure, or to intensive cancer treatment. Joan and Shanin, who were with me, were obviously troubled. Shanin was somewhat relieved to hear the diagnosis of Hodgkin's rather than non-Hodgkin's, which generally carries a worse prognosis. Joan and I both had questions about diet, but different agendas. Joan is an accomplished gourmet cook who attended cooking schools around the world and once ran a school herself. She also once had a pie manufacturing company, but that never impeded her concern for keeping me on a healthy diet, which for her meant low-cholesterol food. All else being equal, I like to eat whatever I want, and I was more pleased than Joan, who was more health food–oriented, to hear Dr. Glick's suggestion: Eat a high-calorie diet, including lots of meat and protein, and do not worry about cholesterol. The important thing was being well nourished.

The day after the house call, February 16, I arrived at the Abramson Cancer Center at the Hospital of the University of Pennsylvania (HUP), where I was to receive my cancer treatments. I was put through a battery of tests, notably tests of heart and lung function and a PET scan, which is designed to look at the metabolism of tumors. While Dr. Glick was reviewing the test results, Joan and I had a conference with Carrie Stricker, a young nurse practitioner who explained the probable course of treatment that awaited me. After a stressful wait that must have been shorter than it seemed, the doctor entered the room with the news: the PET scan indicated the presence of the disease in my neck, chest, abdomen, and spleen, but not in my lungs. The scan also showed what were known as hot spots in my second lumbar vertebrae, a bone in my lower back, and the sacrum, the bone that connects the pelvis to the spine. Upon making that finding, Dr. Glick arranged for an MRI to be taken of my spine that same day, which confirmed the disease to be present in the suspected vertebrae and the sacrum. By midafternoon, with all the test results in hand, Dr. Glick officially made the diagnosis of advanced Hodgkin's disease at Stage IVB.

I asked why I had had been diagnosed at the most advanced stage, and Dr. Glick told me the presence of the disease in the bone made my ailment more advanced than Stage IIIB. The categorization struck me as less than scientific, but I was not going to argue about my diagnosis. The disease was what it was, and dwelling on numbers would not accomplish anything. I was glad finally to discover what was wrong with me.

In retrospect, I believe I had had the symptoms of the disease for at least three months before it was finally diagnosed. Still, the questions filled my mind: What's the mortality rate for Hodgkin's lymphoma? Why was the disease not detected sooner? How long do I have to live? What are the prospects for a cure? I was not much comforted when my doctor told me that if you have to have something bad happen to you, this is the best of the bad things, because Hodgkin's disease is curable. With little time to dwell on these questions, my thoughts turned from my health to the political impact of the public disclosure. I had a sense of the best way to deal with this, because I had been here before.

4

MY HEALTH ODYSSEY

THERE IS AN old saying, "Experience is a hard teacher because she gives the test first, the lesson afterward." It is a corollary to the adage: "Death is nature's way of telling us to slow down." An important lesson I learned or relearned from my experience with Hodgkin's is not to place total reliance on the advice or diagnoses of doctors, even experts. A prudent patient *must* keep asking questions. In my case, the delay in diagnosing Hodgkin's paralleled earlier misdiagnoses of other ailments by other prominent doctors.

In January 1979, when I was approaching my forty-ninth birthday, I experienced unusual pain in my left arm. Following an electroencephalogram at HUP, I was diagnosed with amyatrophic lateral sclerosis (ALS), better known as Lou Gehrig's disease, by a preeminent neurosurgeon. I remember sitting in my hospital room overlooking the university's Franklin Field, where I had seen many college football games three decades earlier, staring at my hands. Were they quivering? They appeared to be; but even at that moment, I thought I might be imagining it. My mind was conjuring symptoms of a neurological disease. I went to the medical library, researched the disease, and learned that life expectancy ranged from two to seven years. Since there was no treatment, let alone a cure, all I could do was wait as the symptoms developed.

Fortunately, none did. By spring, the neurosurgeon reversed his diagnosis and said I did not have ALS. Then why the diagnosis? He sheepishly said an alternative explanation was that I had a mild case of polio as a child that would produce the same electroencephalogram reading. Why, then, didn't he simply tell me at the outset that there might be some other explanation for my symptoms than that I faced a death sentence? The doctor's flustered nonanswer told me a great deal about the limitations of medical expertise, both in diagnosis and in sensitivity toward patients.

My next death sentence occurred fourteen years later. It was a Friday morning, June 11, 1993, and the Senate was not in session. I had been feeling slight pains running down the sides of my head and a tightness in my shirt collars, and the Senate schedule gave me a free morning and an opportunity to get an MRI. Joan was scheduled to arrive in Washington later that day, and we planned to drive to a Virginia inn to celebrate our fortieth wedding anniversary, which was the following Monday. Although the doctors said I did not need an MRI, I insisted, since the procedure was risk-free and noninvasive. I checked into the X-ray unit at Bethesda Naval Hospital at 7:00 A.M. for the forty-five-minute test. When I encountered a long wait afterward for the results, I wondered if something was wrong. Around 11:30, Dr. Robert Krasner, attending physician to Congress, walked in with a troubled expression on his face and said he wanted to take me to see the hospital's chief neurosurgeon. He said nothing further until we entered the office of the chief neurosurgeon, where we found him examining the MRI films. He pointed to a shadow on the film and said it was a tumor the size of a golf ball embedded between my brain and skull. Without any preliminary warning, he said, rather matter-of-factly, it was malignant and I had three to six weeks to live.

In a rambling stream of consciousness, I told the doctor, "My wife is coming down today. We planned to go to Virginia to celebrate our fortieth anniversary."

"Go and have a good time," the neurosurgeon replied. Upon hearing that, I thought, "This guy must be crazy." I instantly doubted his judgment on all counts.

"Give me the MRI films," I said. "I'm going to Philadelphia." I called Joan to inform her only that I had a medical problem and that I would be on the 2:00 P.M. train. Dr. Krasner's chief of staff at the attending physician's office later told me that the doctor was incredulous with my calm response to the diagnosis and almost had a heart attack when I insisted on going to Philadelphia alone on the train.

It was the longest of my many Amtrak rides between Washington and Philadelphia to give Joan the news that our weekend, and perhaps a whole lot more, was ruined. She was stunned. I went straight from the 30th Street Station in Philadelphia to see another neurosurgeon at Jefferson Hospital. He looked at the MRI films and said it was unclear whether the tumor was benign or malignant. I later went home, where I sat in my den making calls to numerous people seeking recommendations for the names of other doctors I could consult. My brother-in-law, Seymour Kety, an accomplished medical scientist in his own right, referred me to Dr. Eugene Flamm, one of the nation's foremost neurosurgeons, at HUP. Dr. Flamm arranged to meet Joan and me on Saturday morning, looked at the films along with a neuroradiologist, and agreed that they were inconclusive. Dr. Flamm scheduled my brain surgery for 7:00 A.M. on Monday morning.

Whatever else was on my mind, I could not help thinking about the political response to the problem of the tumor in my head. This preoccupation grows out of a politician's sense that, whether a candidate or an officeholder, he owes it to constituents to be honest, but to tell the truth in a way that does the least political damage. One's health problems should be discussed with the public with the best possible, albeit accurate, face. Some underemphasize the part about accuracy, but this is foolish. If a politician is not honest, it will be found out eventually, and the deception may grow into a big black mark against his record—perhaps enough to warrant electoral defeat. Before entering the hospital the night before the brain surgery for the tumor in 1993, I walked around the block with Joan to try to take my mind off my problems and enjoy a nice evening in a pleasant neighborhood as best I could. I left it to Shanin to communicate with the press after the operation. I left instructions for Dr. Flamm to tell Shanin the details of the operation after it was completed. That was to be followed by a news release the next day.

When the time came at 7:00 A.M. on June 14, 1993, exactly forty years after Joan and I were married, I was wheeled into an operating room surrounded by bright lights and a phalanx of medics dressed in green. The scene resembled the set of a television medical drama. After the front of my head was shaved, the anesthesia set in, and the next thing I knew, I was in the recovery room at about 10:30 A.M. After about an hour, a hospital attendant wheeled me to my own room. My first request was for a telephone, because I had left Washington abruptly Friday morning with a number of matters that required my attention. I called my office at about 11:45 to speak to my chief of staff about an issue facing the Philadelphia Naval Shipyard, along with two other matters that called for swift action. While I was talking, Dr. Flamm walked in and gave me a look that initially struck me as somewhere between startled and disapproving. After a few moments, his expression gave way to a smile. He apparently thought, "If this guy can be on the telephone so soon after he had his head cut open, he must be okay." The doctor then recounted the gory details. He had used a power saw to cut a 2" by 2" by 2" incision into my skull. He removed the cut-out skull, scooped out the meningioma, put the displaced portion of the skull into its original position, and sewed me up. Years later, the procedure still seems gruesome, but those are the marvels of modern medicine.

That same day, Pennsylvania's governor, Robert Casey, had a double organ transplant in Pittsburgh. The *Philadelphia Daily News* ran the headline "Anguish" above photos of Casey and me, juxtaposed so that each of us was looking at the other. Much of the state government closed that day out of respect, or perhaps more accurately, to speculate. No doubt there was calculation in the state capital of Harrisburg as to who would replace us and who would get their jobs and so forth down the line—but we both recovered.

In order to determine whether the tumor was malignant or benign, it had to be analyzed by pathologists. The meningioma was frozen, sliced down, and microscopically examined the day after surgery. Shanin, who was privy to all the findings, received the report. Late Tuesday morning, he held a news conference with Joan and Dr. Flamm present to advise the media that the tumor was benign and the prognosis was excellent. Dr. Flamm pointed out to reporters, "You must remember that this tumor has been there for, let us say, fifteen years. He's far better off now without it. So I don't see any reason that he

ought to curtail his activities. If anything, he could probably do more."

"Oh, no," Joan chimed in, laughing.[1]

In my first night out after recuperating, Shanin and I
attended what turned out to be an unpredictably long
Philadelphia Phillies game the evening of July 7, 1993. The
team was playing the Dodgers, who sent the game into extra innings by tying the score in the top of the ninth inning. I felt pretty good, so I suggested to Shanin that we
stay a while longer. We kept reassessing the situation as the
game progressed through the tenth, eleventh, twelfth, thirteenth innings and beyond, until we decided that the test
of my stamina would be more interesting than the game.
The Phillies eked out a 7–6 victory in the twentieth inning
at 1:37 A.M., and I lasted the full six hours plus, by far the
team's longest game that year.

My younger son Steve gave me excellent advice: "Listen
to your body, Dad." Since the ALS scare, my internal body
gauges seemed at times more accurate than the specialists
or the high-tech medical tests.[2] In retrospect, I am almost
as disappointed in the team of expert doctors who missed
the correct diagnosis of Hodgkin's for months as I am with
the doctors who made an incorrect diagnosis of ALS and a
malignant brain tumor. It was only when Dr. Glick found
the nodules by feeling the glands under my armpits that it
became apparent that I had Hodgkin's. With expert in-
ternists on the job, and for that matter a string of seven
other doctors whom I saw, looking for nodules under the
armpits should have occurred to someone. Instead it

dragged on from November to February while I was in discomfort, really pained, before the Hodgkin's was diagnosed and I could begin the road to recovery.

After my Hodgkin's diagnosis, Senator Leahy shared a parallel story about his wife, Marcelle. She survived a potentially deadly melanoma by following her own instincts in the face of inept medical advice. For years, her regular physician told her the ten-year-old splotch on the left side of her face was not cancer. Her instincts told her he was wrong. After her doctor retired, she raised the issue with her new doctor, who recommended a biopsy that turned out to show the incipient stage of cancer. She would not have discovered this until she made the decision to get a second, unbiased opinion "outside the group" because, she remarked, doctors tend to "talk to each other and they think similarly." After considerable searching, she finally consulted one of the best cancer surgeons at Johns Hopkins in Baltimore. He operated with the Mohs procedure, an advanced skin cancer treatment that removes cancerous tissue in stages, with intermittent tests, to ensure the malignancy is entirely removed before the patient is released. Senator Leahy remarked that had it not been for his wife's persistence, "she would have died." Marcelle's story, like mine, carries the lesson: Ask questions; don't blindly follow anyone's judgment; and get a second opinion from the best specialist you can find.

I frankly acknowledge that it may be easy for a U.S. senator to tell people without a prestigious position or wealth to seek the best professional help possible. Even in this day and age, socioeconomic status too often remains a barrier to doing so, but there are many generous doctors and hospitals giving excellent medical treatment without limiting services to patients with big bucks or fancy titles. Moreover, technology today permits anyone with access to the Internet to get a head start in self-diagnosis and seeking quality medical care.

Even after my brain surgery in 1993, I would have to put the principle of multiple opinions to the test. In June 1996, an MRI indicated that a smaller brain tumor had returned. This time, almost all the doctors I consulted advised undergoing another surgery. A small minority of specialists recommended the gamma knife, a new technique in which doctors converge radiation beams to destroy small tumors. I made a real effort to study the alternatives. Why did most doctors, even some with extensive experience with the gamma knife, advise conventional surgery? Because that was the traditional approach, since there was more long-term follow-up data on the surgery and the tumor was conveniently located for surgery. The gamma knife, it was argued, should be reserved for locations the surgeon's knife could not reach.

Nonetheless, I consulted some two dozen doctors, including the inventor of the gamma knife in Sweden, and still others in the United States. There was agreement that the gamma knife procedure, even if unsuccessful, would not make it more difficult to treat the tumor with conventional surgery later. Why not avert the potential complications of being cut open? My research led me to opt for this procedure, and I found a doctor with extensive experience with the gamma knife: Dr. Dade Lunsford of the University of Pittsburgh Medical Center.

The procedure was scheduled for October 11, 1996. With the medical decision out of the way, I turned, as before, to the question of how to handle the problem with political sensitivity. I asked doctors to allow me to enter the hospital the morning of the surgery rather than the night before, which was more typical, and quietly arrived at the hospital at 5:30 A.M. After checking in, I had a brace attached to my head, had another MRI, received a local anesthetic, and had pins pressed to my head to secure the brace. The procedure began at 9:30, when my head was inserted into a five-hundred-pound metal helmet with precision holes to allow two hundred cobalt beams from the gamma knife to focus on the regrowth. I was given seven bombardments of radiation for up to three minutes each. In midmorning, while the procedure appeared to be going well, we advised the news media I would hold a 2:30 news conference at the hospital.

The procedure was completed at 10:50 A.M., and after having lunch, I met the Pennsylvania press as scheduled before it knew I had a problem. I was dressed in a brown glen-plaid sports coat, looking as casual and nonchalant as possible. I started the conference by telling the gathered reporters, "We brought you here to tell you about the gamma-knife procedure because we knew you'd be interested. And we thought you'd be less interested if we told you about it than if you found out about it collaterally—understanding the rules of your profession, and ours." "I am fine," I continued, and the treatment had been successful. I then described the gamma knife procedure in detail before quipping: "They served me a big piece of cake, and that's what this day has been, a piece of cake."[3] The *Inquirer* reported, "Senator Arlen Specter looked tired and a little pale, but his voice and handshake were firm."[4] The next day, I scheduled a noon news conference at the Famous Delicatessen in Queens Village, Philadelphia, holding our three-year-old granddaughter Silvi in one arm and our year-old granddaughter Perri in the other to show I was robust and healthy. When you hold public office and anticipate running again, as I did in the 1998 election cycle, the first impressions to follow disclosure of a serious medical problem are very important.

As it turned out, lingering impressions from my brain tumor would be the least of my concerns in 1998. During the 1980s, I had been diagnosed with atrial fibrillation, a condition causing abnormal heartbeat that required me to be on a blood thinner known as coumadin. One Sunday in May 1998, I felt chest pains after shaking hands at an event commemorating Israeli Independence Day at Penn's Landing in Philadelphia. I again felt chest pains while playing squash on Friday, May 29. The following morning, I telephoned my cardiologist, Dr. Howard Weitz. Thirty-one years earlier, he had stuffed envelopes for me as a fourteen-year-old intern in my mayoral campaign office. A preliminary examination in a nearby medical office convinced the doctor that my symptoms demanded immediate care: I had severe heart vessel narrowing. I noted that I was due to make an appearance at Veterans Stadium the following day with Phillies pitcher Curt Schilling. "I don't care about Curt Schilling," Dr. Weitz blurted back. We were going to the hospital that afternoon.

He joined me as I checked into Jefferson Hospital. Not wanting to look feeble in public, I declined the wheelchair offered to me near the entrance, and the two of us walked through the hospital to a patient room. Dr. Weitz told me I needed a cardiac catheterization, but because I had taken a double dose of coumadin the previous day after missing my dose forty-eight hours before, the doctors could not immediately proceed before giving me medicine to reverse the blood thinning. That process would take a day and a half. In the meantime, I mentioned my desire to hold a press conference in the cardiac care unit, but Dr. Weitz replied that that was unacceptable. The catheterization occurred on the morning of June 1, and it revealed two blockages: a 90 percent narrowing of the left anterior descending coronary artery—a condition doctors grimly referred to as the widow maker—and a 70 percent narrowing of an adjacent vessel. Dr. Weitz recommended double bypass surgery to alleviate the blockages. I wanted to seek a second opinion, but the doctor warned that I faced a significant risk of a heart attack if I did not have the procedure immediately. I was reluctant to break my own rule of obtaining a second opinion, but under the circumstances, I felt I had little choice but to assent.

Dr. Richard Edie, the chair of cardiac surgery at the hospital, performed my open-heart operation on the afternoon of June 1. I remained in the hospital for fifteen days recuperating, spending some of it on a ventilator in the cardiac intensive care unit. By June 5, I was heavily medicated, sleep deprived, and delirious, trying to become rational with Joan and my staff, without making much progress. At one point, I called a staff member in Philadelphia to ask him to come by and take me to Bucks County, where I had a lot of work to do. Joan took the phone and gently set the petrified staffer straight. I was a veritable nuisance to hospital staff, and they must have been glad to see me leave. It was the sickest I had ever been, and many people I knew questioned whether I would make it.[5]

Several days after surgery, I developed respiratory distress, probably as a result of my weakened condition and an inability to clear lung secretions. This worsened until June 6, when my heart slowed down, and for a few seconds, stopped beating in the middle of the night. I was given a Code Blue classification, meaning I faced a life-threatening emergency. Medical staff quickly arrived and applied electric paddles to shock my heart into restarting. Dr. Weitz, who was called at his suburban home, told me he broke all speed records driving to Jefferson Hospital. He had me placed on a ventilator, because he thought my heart complications arose from inhaling a fair amount of lung secretions, which slowed my breathing as well. Pneumonia subsequently set in that night. My wife still won't tell me what I said at that time. She does comment, albeit obliquely, about rushing to the hospital at 3:00 A.M. To this day, I vividly recall the nightmares, day and night, as I struggled on a respirator to relieve the congestion caused by the water on my lungs.

During the morning of the seventh, Dr. Edie brought me into surgery to drain my lung fluid. An ultrasound followed to check my heart-pumping function, which turned out to be normal, but a pericardial effusion (fluid collected around the heart) was detected and was impairing my heart's pumping chambers from filling with blood, necessitating another operation by Dr. Edie to drain the fluid. Joan was a real trooper, staying with me at the hospital from 8:30 A.M. to 10:00 P.M. each day. Since she astutely observed that "hospital food is uneatable," she brought me food the last few days of my stay to help me gain strength, a silent reminder of how lucky I was to be married to a gourmet cook. As with my respirator, she asked doctors about the medications I was being given. She stood near my door to guard against the sometimes excessive evening visits from hospital doctors who just wanted to talk to a senator. She discouraged visitors other than our sons and daughter-in-law since I was in no condition to chat. In short, her vigilance provides a model for anyone who has a loved one enter the hospital.

On one occasion, Marc Howard, a reporter for Philadelphia's Channel 6 news, made his way onto my hospital floor in a jogging suit, a contrivance designed to avoid detection, until the hospital staff kicked him out. Shanin subsequently gave Howard a piece of his mind for violating my privacy, and Howard disingenuously tried to cast his "visit" as an act of friendship. We thought he was looking for a story, because rumors were rampant that my death might be imminent.

When I was about to leave the hospital on June 15, the nurses brought me a wheelchair to take me down several long corridors and an elevator to my car. Although I was shaky, I did not want to be seen, let alone be photographed, in a wheelchair. After I reached the last long corridor leading to my car, I left the wheelchair as soon as I was visible to the awaiting photographers and television cameras. Despite my efforts, a haggard-looking picture of me taken that day still appears from time to time in *The Philadelphia Inquirer,* demonstrating that a negative impression can last a long time.

A week after my discharge, Dr. Weitz determined that I was doing "phenomenally well" given my ordeal, and he gave me clearance to resume squash on August 2. After I returned to the Senate in July 1998, I asked David Urban, my chief of staff, to find the largest couch he could for my hideaway office. He dutifully went to an obscure Senate warehouse with a tape measure and came back with a cloth-cushioned couch that he observed was large enough for a nap. I was under doctor's orders to take regular naps, and I did so discreetly. The words of support I received from friends and associates on Capitol Hill were comforting. In one memorable July hearing of the Judiciary Committee, Attorney General Janet Reno ended the proceeding, in which

I had subjected her to some extensive questioning, by asking, "Could I make a personal point?"

"Sure," I replied.

"It is very nice to see you here." That completely disarming statement is the nicest end to a hearing I have ever heard.[6]

All things considered, I was fortunate that in 1998 I faced my only general election for the Senate that did not present a serious possibility of losing. My opponent, Bill Lloyd, while well qualified, was a little-known state representative who raised minimal funds for the race. I made a 100 percent recovery in time to win that November with 61 percent of the vote after spending less than $2 million on radio and television.[7]

Despite my medical history, when Dr. Glick examined me for Hodgkin's, he said he found me young beyond my years. He connected two activities to my vigor: my Senate work and the game of squash. People frequently ask how my squash game is, and my standard answer is "daily." I typically get a surprised reaction, to which I amplify my answer: Yes, I mean seven days a week. Over the years, I had developed a pattern of playing early in the morning on weekdays in Washington and late in the afternoon on weekends in Philadelphia. I rotated with about ten or twelve squash partners in each city. My 7:00 A.M. game had moved to 6:00 or 6:30 as breakfast meetings and some 8:30 hearings required earlier visits to the gym. Admittedly, I occasionally begrudge the time squash occupies during my weekends in Philadelphia, which I consider my personal time to spend playing with my grandchildren or attending sporting events. But then, weekend squash adds to the quantity as well as the quality of my weekends. Even on my Senate travels abroad, I play wherever a squash court is available. I can always find a partner at the embassy or from the marine contingent, or as a last resort, with the local pro. On one ten-day December trip several years ago, I played squash six times—once each in Brussels, Belgium; Riga, Estonia; Amman, Jordan; Frankfurt, Germany; and twice in Tel Aviv, Israel—and headed straight for a squash court as soon as my plane returned to Philadelphia.

Squash is a two-player game played on a four-walled indoor rectangular court using a racquet and rubber ball. In the singles game, which I typically play, a proper "rally," as it is known, begins as the players take turns hitting the ball against the designated zone on the front wall. After the server first strikes the ball, the receiving player may hit it on the fly or after one bounce, but before it bounces twice. Following the serve, the ball may hit any of the three other walls before it hits the designated zone of the front wall. The rally continues until a player is unable to return the other's shot, which gives the other player a point. Each game typically goes to fifteen points under the American scoring system, and a match is determined by the best of five games.

Squash provides a good workout and helps keep the mind sharp. Because there are many strategies to the game, the player can focus on speed or emphasize ball placement. One of my regular squash partners, Tom Worrall, aptly described squash as the chess of racquet sports. Precision is essential to winning the game. And a certain competitive edge that has driven me in politics stays with me on the squash court. Senator John Chafee of Rhode Island was a regular squash partner in my early Senate days, and he once asked me early in 1983 how I thought I had done against him during the previous year. I thought I beat him pretty handily, but replied, "Oh, I think we broke about even." He then said that he reported the scores to his secretary every day, "and she says I beat you last year."

"Like hell you did, Chafee," I retorted. I was sure he was wrong, and his statement motivated me to keep track each day of the name of my opponent and games won and lost. I have dutifully kept track of every squash match in my datebook for the subsequent twenty-five years.

Nowadays, on weekdays in Washington, I use the squash courts at the Federal Reserve building—the only available building I know of with a court for hardball, the version of squash I play. In Philadelphia, I use the court at the Sporting Club adjacent to the Bellevue-Stratford Hotel. My usual squash partners are between their thirties and fifties in age. My most frequent partner the year I was diagnosed with Hodgkin's was Evan Kelly, a thirty-one-year-old Judiciary Committee counsel. He moved like a gazelle on the squash court, but I kept our games competitive by running him all over the court while I stayed in the center at what is called the T. And no, he was adamant that he did not let me win simply because he worked for me. I began playing Evan when he was twenty-nine, and when he turned thirty, I informed him his advantage had disappeared. I have added that he may have a chance to win more often when he is half my age, but he has had a hard time calculating precisely when that will occur.

I used to say that squash was the most important thing I did each day. Now I say it is the only important thing I do every day. I analogize my squash games to trips to the health bank. Each match, each game, and each point is a deposit in the bank. Playing virtually every day since October 1970 has given me a sizable reserve fund of health credits. I have drawn from that reserve through my many illnesses, and it has taken many credits in the bank to cover all of my health challenges. Squash may well have been a lifesaver during my many medical ordeals.

In the difficult weeks before my Hodgkin's diagnosis, I had tried my best to maintain a daily squash schedule. I sometimes fell short, but played as late as the day before my seventy-fifth birthday, just prior to my diagnosis. I relished playing the game just as I relished any good challenge. The game is conducive to unlikely comebacks. I could not count the number of matches in which one player seemed to be hopelessly trailing, only to catch up through tenacity and ultimately win the match. I often tell my opponents, "Squash is a great lesson for life: You're never too far behind to win, and you're never too far ahead to lose."

This was true as well of other challenges, be they political or medical. My history with death sentences, all of them fortunately inaccurate, undoubtedly prepared me to take on Hodgkin's. It gave me a sense of confidence that tough or even seemingly hopeless battles can be won. I would deal with this simply by going about my business, which now included the work in the Senate I had hoped to do for so long. To do any less was unthinkable. Whether the challenge has been medical or political, I have believed in Winston Churchill's mantra: "Never give in, never give in, never, never, never."

5

FACING TREATMENT, BUT NOT ALONE

GIVEN THAT MY Hodgkin's diagnosis followed two grueling years on an exhausting reelection campaign, not to mention a demanding Senate schedule, it is no surprise why I speculate on the extent to which the accompanying stress of my life caused my affliction. My own experience does make me think that stress is a contributing factor, but it is difficult to say how much so, next to aging and the physical exhaustion that comes with hard work. I try not to dwell on such questions since they concern what cannot be changed. My simple doctrine has been that what is, is. Determine what you *can* control or influence, and move on.

After Dr. Glick diagnosed me with Hodgkin's, my mind quickly turned for guidance to how I had handled the news media during past illnesses. Granted, my next potential election was five years and nine months away, and a reelection campaign at age eighty was speculative in any event, but that is where my mind drifted. In contemplating how to break the news of my diagnosis, I knew the disclosure must be very prompt and minutely accurate. If someone else broke the story before I did, that would leave the impression of a cover-up. If minimized, even innocently, again there might be the same innuendo.

At the same time, it was essential to call my sisters, aunts, and staff members so that they would not hear the news from the press first. My thinking was, in part, a reaction to two considerably different incidents that left an impression on me. First, I thought of the day in 1991 when Senator John Heinz, the senior senator from Pennsylvania during my first decade in the Senate, died tragically and unexpectedly. Senator Heinz and six other people were killed when his plane collided with a helicopter that was attempting to investigate a mechanical issue on the wheels of his plane. A relative of mine in Chicago heard a radio news headline announcing that a Republican senator from Pennsylvania was killed in a plane crash, which naturally led him to believe I was dead. In a very different context, my son Shanin learned on his car radio while driving through Philadelphia that his mother had just been slated to run for the Philadelphia city council. At the first available moment, he called her to ask, "I've had to explain my father for years, and now you too? Why did I have to hear about it on the radio?" The reason was that Bill Meehan, the Republican leader in Philadelphia, had asked her to run at the last minute, and her papers had to be filed immediately. Thus, I took particular caution with respect to this particular disclosure.

The reaction to the news of my diagnosis was typically shock, especially among those who had been with me through the political challenges of the previous year. Alison Cooper, then my deputy chief of staff, became emotional: "Senator, I'm so sorry. I'm so sorry. It's just not fair. You're finally chairman of the Judiciary Committee." Bettilou Taylor, who managed my appropriations subcommittee staff, pursued Dr. Elias Zerhouni, director of the NIH, early in the morning in search of an additional medical assessment. NIH physicians are available for consultation by all Americans at all times with a simple phone call. They had helped many of my constituents, and they were there for me when I needed them. Bettilou arranged an afternoon conference call with Dr. Zerhouni, Dr. Wyndham Wilson, who directed the lymphoma research branch of NIH, Dr. Glick, Joan, and me. We reviewed the voluminous information that had been compiled on my condition, and the NIH doctors agreed that the chemotherapy treatment proposed by Dr. Glick was the way to go. Joan asked about herbal and other alternative treatments, but Dr. Wilson was strongly against it.

Later that afternoon, my staff met in the conference room in my Washington office with the Pennsylvania district offices phoned in to convey the news to everyone who worked for me. I was not there, but I am told the reaction to the news, relayed by David Brog, was a stunned silence. Gayle Mills, the director of one of my Pennsylvania offices, listening via her car phone, ran her car off the road, fortunately without any injury or damage. Bettilou distributed a batch of Lance Armstrong bracelets. The small yellow bands, inscribed with the slogan "LiveStrong," were developed by the world-renowned cyclist and cancer survivor as a way to show solidarity with cancer victims and advocate more funding for cancer research.

Avoiding a chance bacterial infection became an immediate goal. David purchased a large Purell hand sanitizer for the office and encouraged staffers to make use of it to minimize the chances that I might become infected. When meeting people, I would follow my doctor's orders by cutting down on handshaking and reverting to slaps on the back, but it is impossible for a politician to suspend handshaking altogether. This would prove true even at a fund-raiser for Senator Santorum about a month later, where I walked into a room full of doctors who had put their hands in their pockets to discourage me from shaking hands.

I did not have much time to speak with colleagues on what was shaping up to be a day as frenetic in pace as any workday, but Bettilou made calls to a number of senators on my behalf. One senator I did get to speak with that day was Tom Harkin of Iowa, the ranking member of the appropriations subcommittee I chaired. Expressing shock, he offered to come up to see me, but I said it wasn't necessary and outlined the treatments I would receive.

"Well," he responded, "can we do anything about that?"

"No, I'll be okay," I replied.

"Well, how long are you going to be gone from the Senate?"

"Oh, I'm not going to be gone from the Senate."

"What? You could do this?" Tom fired back.

"Yeah, I can do this," I said as matter-of-factly as I could. That Hodgkin's would not curtail my work was one message the public would have to know.

By the late afternoon of Wednesday, February 16, I had been observed at both Jefferson Hospital and HUP, and press inquiries were mounting. It was time to pull the facts together and put them on paper. Shanin had amassed extensive experience with the news media over the course of my political career, and his law practice, which focused heavily on medical malpractice cases, gave him considerable medical expertise. Having dealt with my past illnesses, he knew exactly what to do. Besides, I consider him the best political mind in the country. If he ever ran for public office, people would see why. With extensive input from Dr. Glick, he meticulously drafted a comprehensive statement for the press for a 5:00 P.M. release. The first Associated Press wire would appear less than twenty minutes after the statement went out. The release detailed my symptoms, the tests of the last several days, and the course of treatment. It also was explicit about the advanced stage of my cancer. I did not have much knowledge of cancer staging, but Shanin explained that if we remained silent about the stage, people would assume I suffered from the most severe stage anyway. My good will could remain intact only if the people heard the news from us directly, fully, and immediately.

Dr. Glick had pointed out that, with my illness, there generally was a 75 percent chance of complete response, or complete remission, for recipients of chemotherapy, and about an 80 percent chance of surviving five years— the point at which the patient is considered cured. In drafting the release, my five-year survival rate was lowered by Dr. Glick and Shanin to 70 percent due to my age. With that adjustment, the press statement was issued. It read as follows:

Philadelphia, PA — Senator Arlen Specter today announced that he has been diagnosed with Hodgkin's disease. Hodgkin's disease is a cancer of the lymph system. Approximately 7500 new cases are diagnosed every year in the United States.

Senator Specter had experienced persistent fevers and enlarged lymph nodes under his left arm and above his left clavicle. He received testing on February 14th at Thomas Jefferson University Hospital. The testing involved biopsy of a lymph node and biopsy of bone marrow. The lymph node was positive for Hodgkin's disease. The bone marrow biopsy showed no cancer. A follow up PET scan and MRI at the Abramson Cancer Center of the University of Pennsylvania on February 16th established that Senator Specter has stage IVB Hodgkin's disease.

Senator Specter is expected to receive ABVD chemotherapy every two weeks over the next 24 to 32 weeks at the Abramson Cancer Center.

It is expected that Senator Specter will be able to perform all duties of his office including those related to the chairmanship of the Judiciary Committee.

Senator Specter's oncologist, John H. Glick, M.D., said: "Senator Specter has an excellent chance of being completely cured of his Hodgkin's disease. Senator Specter's Hodgkin's disease has a five-year survival rate of 70%. He is in superb physical condition, particularly in light of his daily squash regimen." Dr. Glick is Professor of Medicine at Penn and a nationally renowned expert in Hodgkin's disease.

Senator Specter said: "I have beaten a brain tumor, bypass heart surgery and many tough political opponents; and I'm going to beat this too. I have a lot more work to do for Pennsylvania and America."

Exhausted, I went home for a long night's sleep and returned to HUP Thursday morning for what the doctors called minor, outpatient surgery to insert a round, metallic object called a "port" into the upper right side of my chest, about three inches beneath my clavicle. The port was about two inches in diameter with a twelve-inch tube descending into a large vein. It was covered by a rubber diaphragm through which a needle could be inserted. This would enable fluids to be injected into my system during my biweekly chemotherapy treatments and periodic tests. It was the safest and most workable option for me, because veins on both of my arms had taken a beating over the years from numerous tests to determine my coumadin level, or blood thinness. I felt completely battered that day, and I resigned myself to whatever the doctors ordered. My life seemed out of my hands. No discussion; no arguments; just do what the doctor says. At some other time, one could inquire and make some decisions, but not then.

As I was prepared for treatment, the Judiciary Committee held the only markup in the 109th Congress to occur without me. I asked Senator Hatch to chair the hearing in my absence, and he graciously made several pleas to the members to report the bankruptcy reform bill out to the full Senate "for Arlen." Not that this was an easy task. Orrin tried to get members to limit the time they took to speak, but several members on the Democratic side were disinclined to cooperate as they offered a number of amendments. Senator Hatch deftly indulged them while discouraging Republicans from taking too much time themselves, which allowed the bill to be reported out successfully. After the markup, my staff gathered for another meeting, and I addressed them by phone with a survey of treatments I would receive and reassurances I would remain Judiciary chairman. In fact, I would surprise many in the Senate by returning in time for floor debate and passage of the bankruptcy reform bill—the first major legislation to become law in the 109th Congress when the president signed it on February 18.

My Senate colleagues were sympathetic and supportive of me without exception. Senator Hatch was consistently upbeat about my ability to beat the disease, and Senator Frist displayed more of the subdued watchfulness one would expect from someone who had practiced medicine. Senator Leahy told me that if there were any days I wanted to keep Judiciary Committee proceedings short, I should just let him know, and he would talk to committee Democrats to get their cooperation. He and his wife, Marcelle, showed great concern about my health. When I saw Marcelle, a registered nurse, she would greet me with a hug— "just checking on my patient," she would say—and I would call her "my favorite nurse." Like Marcelle, the most junior senator on the Judiciary Committee, Dr. Tom Coburn, was a cancer survivor—he had actually survived both colon cancer and melanoma—and he was one of the few nonlawyers on the committee. That he and I were on opposite ends of the political spectrum in the Republican conference did not preclude a warm relationship. As a practicing physician, he was like a second doctor to me, keeping tabs on my progress. He would say that dealing with cancer is "70 percent attitude, 30 percent physicians."

Tom also brought an outspokenness and independence to his job that made him a fascinating addition to the Senate. During the debate over the asbestos bill, he offered many interesting ideas to challenge conventional thinking on the subject of medical causation. He proposed a number of measures that would be added to the bill to increase protection against fraudulent claims of causation. On budgetary matters, he challenged all earmarks—the practice by which individual lawmakers direct appropriations to specific projects of their choosing. Although I did not agree with many of his ideas, I welcomed that level of courage and independence to the Senate.

The immediate aftermath of my diagnosis included news stories that gave me more pessimistic projections than my doctor's survival prognosis of 70 percent. Any so-called expert could get his name in the newspapers by painting a bleaker picture. Herman Kattlove, a doctor affiliated with the American Cancer Society, told *USA Today* I had a 50 percent to 60 percent chance to recover.[1] Dr. Witold Rybka, chief of hematology and oncology at the Penn State Milton S. Hershey Medical Center, told the Harrisburg *Patriot-News:* "Seventy percent is high, even for a twenty-year-old with IVB," and gave me a 35 percent survival rate over five years.[2] I noted these observations as I would an amusing plotline in a *Saturday Night Live* sketch, but I otherwise paid no attention to them. The predictions reminded me of how I was initially written off in the press after my 1993 brain surgery. These gratuitous comments confirmed my suspicions about doctors who diagnose from afar without knowing the patient or most of the facts.

In 1993 too, there was open conjecture among power brokers and office seekers as to who would replace me. Aspirants for my Senate seat, anticipating my demise, were circling like vultures. The Harrisburg *Patriot-News* quoted Governor Ed Rendell saying he was "irate" over so many inquiries as to whom he would appoint in my place. The governor later explained,

When the news broke that Arlen had cancer, I must have gotten five or six calls in the next 24 hours from prominent people saying, "I don't mean to be ghoulish, but if anything happens to Arlen, I'd like to be considered for his Senate seat." I said, "Guys, first, the guy is my friend and he gave me my first job, so you shouldn't be calling me with this. But more important, Arlen's going to outlive all of us." They're going to have to carry him out of the Senate. He'll be a senator into his 80s, and he'll be as energetic then as he is now.[3]

Notwithstanding our different party affiliations, Rendell and I had a good working relationship and were longstanding friends since I gave him his first job out of law school— assistant district attorney—in 1967. For many years, we lived four doors from each other in Philadelphia. When I was diagnosed, the governor's wife, Marjorie, a judge who served on the Third Circuit with the ailing Ed Becker, told her husband, "Leave it to Arlen. He had to one-up Eddie."

Still, as Mark Twain remarked upon the accidental publication of his obituary, reports of my death were greatly exaggerated. This is not to overlook that many newspapers downplayed the unfavorable odds and predicted my survival. The *Pittsburgh Post-Gazette* noted my earlier triumphs over a brain tumor and heart bypass surgery and said that while my prediction of not having the disease interfere with my Senate work "might be wishful thinking in anyone else . . . Senator Specter has stayed remarkably fit by playing squash regularly and is a fighter by nature."[4] Adopting the same theme, the *Philadelphia Daily News* ran an editorial entitled "Senator Fighter" in which it commented: "He'll beat this. The guy is a born fighter."[5] Considering that that newspaper's editorial column seldom had a good word to say about me, that should have concerned me about my chances. A columnist with the paper amusingly did declare, "I say until Specter's office issues a statement reading, 'U.S. Senator Arlen Specter today had a wooden stake driven through his heart,' everybody can just fuhgettaboudit."[6] That could not quite be confused with a pre-obituary courtesy.

The most poignant reaction to my diagnosis came from my granddaughters. Toward the end of *Passion for Truth,* I wrote that I want to leave them my parents' "legacy of optimism, tenacity, and service. As my parents did for me, I want to leave them a better world, a brighter future, and challenges worthy of their gifts."[7] More than anyone else, they remind me what I have to live for. They associated cancer with death after losing Paula Kline, the first person close to them they had lost. As eleven-year-old Silvi put it, Paula was "really caring, nice, and she always listened to all you had to say," and she was "really scared" to hear I was diagnosed with the same illness that claimed her friend. My seven-year-old granddaughter Lilli, who was named after my mother, took my Hodgkin's diagnosis the hardest. In a voice that only a granddaughter can capture, she told me, "I love you. I don't mean I just like you. I mean, I really love you." She then declared that when she grew up, she was going to become a nurse. Her nine-year-old sister

Perri was startled to hear about my projected 70 percent chance to live five years. Her fears seemed allayed when I explained that was the average response, and I expected to do much better because of my fit physical condition. When Silvi encountered the 70 percent figure researching the story on a computer, she said she "felt a lot better," but not without wondering, "What about the 30 percent?" To me, though this might sound irrational, the numbers were a statistical abstraction. They had nothing to do with me. I felt invulnerable, and although I spent many days feeling tired and listless, I never allowed myself to feel down.

I was also motivated to speak with my older sisters, Hilda and Shirley. They are both women of deep faith who were among the first to convey to me what I would hear from so many well-wishers: that I was in their prayers. My sisters maintained a quiet confidence that I would be well, and we all drew strength from the many prayers that were said throughout the Jewish community and beyond. Shirley passed along my Hebrew name, Avraham ben Aron, to friends of her children so that they could gather a minyan, a quorum of ten or more adult males convened for communal prayer, in synagogue. My nephew, Stewart Kety, visited the Western Wall in Jerusalem the Monday after my diagnosis and said a *mishebayrach,* a prayer for the sick. Shanin fielded numerous inquiries from others for my Hebrew name in order to offer prayers in Hebrew on my behalf.

Meanwhile, my office was inundated with calls, letters, faxes, and e-mails from friends going back to grammar and high school days—in addition to numerous constituents I had never met. One sent an endearing get-well message in the form of a stuffed animal. I was moved to read the sentiment expressed by Terry Slease, who had married Carey Lackman in her last days: "You were there for us—We are here for you." Among the callers was President Bush, who had words of cheer and added, "You're a tough guy, Arlen, and we expect you to beat this."[8] Privately, he told friends that he thought about the friendship we had developed during all our trips on Air Force One, so he was concerned primarily about "a friend being very sick" and secondarily about my chairmanship of "an important committee." Bob Dole wrote in, "Arlen, Hang in there. They can't keep the Russell boys down." Another former Senate colleague, Fritz Hollings of South Carolina, added, "Arlen—You can beat this one too! You have to, because you're the only Constitutional mind left." Former New York City mayor Ed Koch wrote, "You have so many more challenges to take on before God calls you home." Other messages had dietary advice, including this from Helen W. Drutt English, founder of a Philadelphia craft gallery whose son survived Hodgkin's: "Crushed garlic and fresh vegetable juices build the immune system and provides you with strength. Stay away from preserved meats and fish, salt, sugar, liquor, white flour and red meats. Steam those vegetables with Joan in the kitchen." Perhaps the most unique letter I received was from TV commentator Armstrong Williams, who wrote, "God is too wise to make a mistake and too just to do wrong."

One of my memorable phone calls was with Donald Cohan, a fellow Philadelphia lawyer my age who came to the bar with me in the mid-1950s. An occasional squash partner in past years, Don is an amazing man of many talents who had won the 1972 Olympic bronze medal in sailing at the age of forty-two. He had a history of health problems that eerily resembled mine: He had suffered from the same kind of benign brain tumor and overcame Hodgkin's disease twice after becoming one of the unusual cases of late recurrence. His initial diagnosis was also IVB, and he was also treated by Dr. Glick. He needed all his competitive spirit to defeat the disease, but his point was a sobering one: "Arlen, you're not in control here. This is one of the few times in your life that you cannot control things." He described his fatigue, nausea, night sweats, and underarm glandular swelling and pain. I was especially concerned about Don's warning of the potential effect of the medication prednisone, which could impair judgment and the ability to make major decisions.

Don's principal advice was twofold: (1) rest when you can; and (2) you're going to be pounded, so keep a record of how you feel through each treatment. As you notice that the pattern is cyclical, it will prevent you from being discouraged during the low points. Don's most dramatic commentary involved pain so severe that he had to get down on his knees, hunched over with his head on a footstool to get momentary relief. On a couple of occasions, he was so sick that he would stick his head in the toilet, laughing and flushing until his wife came in to see what was going on: "Laugh, that's all you can do." His philosophy was "Be the same guy when they're putting an Olympic medal around your neck as when you're throwing up from the chemo. Be true to yourself." In that vein, "Just be Arlen. Don't get a wig or wear a hat. Be who you are and do what you have to do. . . . Get up in front of the television cameras and look as crappy as you look." That last piece of advice was as unnecessary as it was true, because it stated perfectly my philosophy.

Chemotherapy treatments were set for every other Friday so that I could return Monday without missing work. During the 109th Congress, Senate votes usually did not begin earlier than Monday afternoons and usually did not end later than Friday mornings. The Friday following my diagnosis, February 18, would mark my first treatment. Before going, I received a call early in the morning from an old friend, Kathy Kiele, who wanted an exclusive interview for her paper, *USA Today*. She always had treated me well going back to 1980, when she was a cub reporter for the now-defunct *Pittsburgh Press*. The interview was a good warm-up for my first Hodgkin's news conference, scheduled for 10:00 A.M. in HUP and to be attended by eleven TV cameras and all the local print media. I wanted the press corps to see that I was in command of all my faculties when I began the first of twelve chemotherapy treatments one hour later. Based on my conversations with Dr. Glick and my own disposition, I thought I could beat Hodgkin's and decided to be bullish. With some calculation, my sound bite repeated the closing line of my earlier written statement: "I beat a brain tumor, bypass surgery, and many tough political opponents, and I'm going to beat Hodgkin's lymphoma cancer, too." For a little levity at the end, I added: "I plan to cut back to a seventy-hour week promptly."[9]

Accompanied by Joan, I then went to the designated room in the Abramson Cancer Center for my first treatment and took my seat in a large cushioned chair. The room was small, but it had windows wide enough to give me a good view of Franklin Field, the impressive stadium on the University of Pennsylvania campus, and the downtown Philadelphia skyline. I asked the nurse, Marie Walton, if it would be all right if I turned my chair around to take in the view of my beloved city, and she was more than happy to do so before preparing the needle. My chemotherapy entailed a regimen of what Dr. Glick called a "cocktail" known as ABVD—abbreviated for the chemical compounds adriamycin, bleomycin, vinblastine, and dacarbazine—that would be administered intravenously through the port in my chest. Having been acquainted with more pleasant cocktails, the term surprised me. Aside from the needle prick, there was no pain involved in the hour-long procedure. There was a momentary warm or flushing sensation as the cocktail, really a gruesome set of chemical substances, went into a twelve-inch line extending into the veins in my chest. Where it all ultimately went I do not know.

Following that procedure, I received a shot called Aranesp in my upper left arm to increase my red blood hemoglobin count and prevent anemia. In the early days of treatment for Hodgkin's, many patients required transfusions rather than a drug to restore an adequate red blood count. My blood was monitored frequently to be certain my red and white blood counts were satisfactory, as well as my platelet count. That count measured clotting capacity and potential toxicity in bone marrow.

Dr. Glick's capable team, particularly nurses Marie Walton and Carrie Stricker, made the process as smooth as possible. Marie, who actually administered the cocktail, remarked I was "upbeat most of the time," and she certainly helped. Whenever Joan and I came to my room, my chair stood facing the window view of the city, just as I had requested during my first treatment. In stark contrast to my feelings when I stood in the same hospital with a similar view after being misdiagnosed with Lou Gehrig's disease, it was soothing to watch the Schuylkill River, Penn's Franklin Field, the trains arriving at the 30th Street Station, the cars on the Schuylkill Expressway, and the skyline from west to east. When I wasn't reading the newspaper, making phone calls, or speaking with Joan and Dr. Glick, who were usually in the room with me, I looked out at the city and had nostalgic discussions of my past—the Warren Commission, my days as district attorney, my unsuccessful and successful Senate runs.

Carrie's role was to minimize the toxicity of the treatments as well as other side effects and to aim for the highest quality of life. She was a caring nurse who possessed keen awareness of the psychological dimension of the cancer experience. Some patients, she once said, undertake a review of their lives during their illnesses, and my nostalgic reminiscences may well have been such an example. When it came to side effects, I was impressed to see how far cancer treatment had come. Until recently, nausea and vomiting were part and parcel of chemotherapy, but my cocktail included a steroid called Decadron that helps prevent this symptom and increases energy. Although I would emerge from treatments feeling woozy and occasionally felt pangs of nausea, I never vomited during my Hodgkin's experience.

Still, fatigue took a heavy toll on me. There was a rhythm to how I felt that tracked the day of the biweekly treatment cycle. By sleeping for nine or ten hours each night, plus afternoon naps over the weekend after each Friday treatment, I felt pretty well until Sunday or Monday morning, which typically marked the low point. That is when a heavy fatigue would set in and last for most of the week until Friday or Saturday. Then I usually would improve the second week.

From my first chemotherapy treatment on Friday the eighteenth, I was determined not to coddle myself, but to maintain my regular schedule. Joan and I dined that evening with Julia and Steve Harmelin. Before he was my campaign treasurer, Steve had helped me in innumerable endeavors since my mayoral run in 1967, when we first met. Steve was part of an intellectual team I organized that year in a determined effort to wrest the mayor's office in a city controlled by entrenched, complacent Democrats. The team produced fifteen Blueprints for a Better Philadelphia on a variety of issues facing the city, and Steve wrote the Blueprint dedicated to the environment. My first foray in the area of asbestos came in 1971, after Steve pointed out the dangers of the "white stuff" we noticed being sprayed into the air coating the steel girders as a fire prevention measure as a high-rise office building was being constructed across the street from my office in City Hall. The asbestos filled the air and entered my office through the fan on my window air conditioner. Steve told me about the research that was developing on the dangers of asbestos inhalation. I asked the city's Department of Licenses and Inspections to stop the asbestos from being sprayed into downtown Philadelphia. After encountering the agency's indolence, I filed a criminal complaint in my capacity as district attorney under an 1860 Pennsylvania nuisance statute naming the construction contractor as the defendant. After a preliminary hearing, which I personally prosecuted, and after the defendant company was held for action of the grand jury, they stopped spraying the asbestos into the air by enclosing the building at a reported cost of $10 million. That was a precedent to stop such asbestos spraying in Philadelphia and elsewhere.

Back in 1967, Steve was a recent arrival at Dilworth Paxson, a major Philadelphia law firm; and four decades later, he was its managing partner. He has a warm personality and a hilarious sense of humor, which made for a lighthearted dinner, which I needed. My illness was on all our minds, but never explicitly discussed. It tacitly came up once, when Steve handed me a baseball cap that we all understood would come in handy as I lost my hair. "I don't know what I'm going to do," I told him. That decision still awaited me. I later learned that Julia, who had seen a husband succumb to cancer, could not believe how nonchalantly I approached chemo. I did not realize what lay ahead.

The next morning after our dinner, Saturday the nineteenth, I received a house call from Dr. Weitz, my cardiologist, and Dr. Merli, my internist. Both appeared a bit sheepish, I surmised because they had not detected the Hodgkin's earlier. Both are superb professionals who had always been available to me day or night, weekends or holidays, to the point that I felt pampered. They measured my coumadin level and gave me a thorough examination. They were satisfied with what they observed and seemed relieved that I was in good spirits. Dr. Weitz said I had tolerated chemo so well, "it was as if nothing had happened." Notwithstanding a little headache and more than a little fatigue, Joan and I decided to get some air. We drove to visit our grandchildren that afternoon in the suburbs and then did some shopping at Nordstrom's in the nearby King of Prussia mall.

Later that afternoon, a nurse made a house call to show me how to inject Neulasta, a substance that would boost my white blood cell count to help prevent infection. The shot entailed sticking a needle into my abdomen. This would be repeated every other Saturday following the chemotherapy cocktail from the day before. I had some experience with self-injection from the times I had taken a coumadin substitute. It was not much fun, but I learned to do what I had to do. Joan found it more painful to administer the needle than I did, so I kidded her by saying I was both the injector and injectee. She could not watch.

We were determined to maintain our social schedule that February weekend, despite approaching fatigue. So Joan and I went out for Saturday dinner with old friends Evelyn and Ed Rosen. I had known Ed since the 1950s from a Jewish fraternal organization. Our Sunday dinner companions were two other longstanding friends, Gail and Peter Hearn. Peter, who had served on my mayoral campaign team with Steve Harmelin, had written my Blueprint for a Better Philadelphia on education. He recalled that the document, with three to four footnotes per page, met a level of scholarship unheard-of for a political position paper, though I like to think of it as standard Specter fare.

Those dinners kept my spirits up and made me forget Hodgkin's for a while. My friends and I customarily react to each other's illnesses without dwelling on them. Ed Rosen had been diagnosed with prostate cancer a dozen years earlier, and I called him at the time to offer the name of a specialist. Immediately after I was diagnosed with Hodgkin's, Ed called me to offer his help. We were there for each other, but we also realized the value of focusing our attention away from illness. The one visible sign of my condition during my weekend dinners was my inability, on my doctor's advice, to hug or kiss my friends, or even to shake hands when people approached me. This was a precautionary measure, arising from the increased risk of infection that often accompanies cancer treatment.

Joan kept a small container of hand sanitizer with her. The dinner conversations, however, focused entirely on life rather than death, and none of my friends from my young adulthood would have had it any other way.

There was, after all, enough time to ponder the unpleasantness. The diagnosis of Hodgkin's began a strange new chapter of my life filled with uncertainty, apprehension, and—yes—fear. Seventy percent sounds like good odds until you realize that the thirty-percent prospect is death. I had given thought to that morbid subject since the age of five, which I acknowledge without knowing precisely why I would have thought about it at such a young age. When I was twelve, I saw a corpse for the first time— the father of Tom Harvey, a friend in my eighth-grade class. I shared in the sadness of the occasion but was revolted by the sight, which remains crisp in my memory six and a half decades later.

As I became older, I was struck by my own father's courage when his life was on the line. Harry Specter grew up in a village in the heart of Ukraine, where he shared a one-room hut with a dirt floor with his parents, seven brothers, and one sister. His earliest impressions were of anti-Semitism and abuse by the Russian government. At the age of eighteen, he saved a few rubles, walked across the European continent, and sailed to America in steerage. He eventually made his way to Kansas, where he sold blankets to the farmers in the winter and cantaloupes on the streets of small towns in the summer.

In 1918, as World War I raged in Europe, he joined the

American Expeditionary Force in France as a buck private. The reality was that he, like so many others, was sent to France so that he could be cannon fodder. He may as well have had an enormous bull's-eye painted on his back. Yet he patriotically brushed that off and was proud to serve in the army of his adopted country. Fighting in the Argonne Forest, he was seriously wounded in action by shrapnel fire. He carried shrapnel in his legs until the day he died and would walk with a limp. It was not only his courage that was memorable, but also his selfless devotion to family, his unflinching optimism, and his ardent work ethic. During the Bonus March of 1932, he shared the outrage of veterans who were marching on Washington to demand the immediate payment of promised bonuses to World War I veterans, bonuses that were not set to be paid until 1945. I have long said that I came to Washington to collect my father's bonus. It has struck me that had the shrapnel hit him a little higher, Harry Specter might have lain in one of the veterans' cemeteries in Europe, and he would not have been my father, and I would not have been. But of course, he was my father, and my hero. He was buried in Israel, as was long his wish, after dying there suddenly of a heart attack while on vacation. Over the course of my frequent travels to the Middle East, I have visited his grave twenty-five times. In 2006, I paid a visit with Veterans Committee members to World War I and World War II cemeteries in the Netherlands and France. The vision of so many marble crosses and marble Stars of David in symmetrical rows was poignant. We know the history of warfare and the casualties it incurs, but until one actually sees the tombstones, the true cost is an abstraction. It is sobering to reflect on the many soldiers in my father's generation who never came home.

My father encountered the natural death that awaits most of us, but my closest association with unnatural death was also (apart from war) the most poignantly remembered death of my generation: the assassination of President Kennedy. I learned the news as I headed back to the D.A.'s office from lunch with a 2:00 P.M. court hearing scheduled in a highly publicized murder case. The president's death made quite an impression on me, not only because he was my president, but because of the admiration I had for him. I considered myself a JFK Democrat at the time, and I was caught up in the mystique of Camelot.[10] I did not expect my career would intersect with the assassination, but I was ready to contribute to the investigation to determine what really happened. When I began my work with the Warren Commission, I read the autopsy report while on a train and grew sick to my stomach reviewing the details of how this vibrant, brilliant young president had been so brutally cut down. I still shudder when I think about it.

John Heinz was another dashing and youthful politician who was taken too soon. We began as primary opponents for the Senate in 1976, but since then had become good friends and members of the upper body's centrist ranks. I heard the news of his fatal plane crash while I was having lunch in New York with David Garth, who had handled campaigns for both of us over the years, and was shocked. I took the earliest opportunity to comfort Senator Heinz's staff in Washington. I wanted to ensure that all were taken care of and invited several of his staffers to come work with me, including Carey Lackman.

Shortly after my Hodgkin's diagnosis, I talked to Rabbi Jay M. Stein, senior rabbi of Har Zion Temple in Penn Valley outside Philadelphia. That temple is my family's principal place of worship, and Rabbi Stein has been a capable steward of the temple, not to mention a caring friend, for three years. Shanin, the rabbi, and I remember our conversation a little differently, and I would defer to their recollections because the subject of mortality is one I prefer not to ponder. We discussed the issues surrounding my illness with Joan and Shanin present, and we agree that no one—least of all I—ever thought that my mortality was an issue. Shanin and the rabbi recall I broached the issue indirectly, asking what Judaism had to say about the afterlife. Rabbi Stein responded with a discussion of several different possibilities acknowledged by the traditions of the faith. One possibility entailed living with God in heaven immediately after death—the automatic result of a virtuous life. Second, for those with a sufficient degree of evil on their shoulders, was the prospect of going initially to an "in-between" place, a concept often described as purgatory, for a period of up to a year before being with God. The third possibility was that all ends at death with nothing to follow. I do not recall what, if anything, I had to say in response, but to Shanin and Rabbi Stein, I appeared satisfied with what I was told.

An illness like Hodgkin's serves as a reminder that we have a limited time—and how our time can end when we least expect it. Moreover, the event of death could never eclipse what is most important, which is how we spend the time we have. In my case, I put thoughts of death out of my mind, but was apprehensive and even fearful of the cumulative ill effects of my treatment. Shanin warned me I would progressively feel worse, and I was apprehensive about being incapacitated. Still, he, his wife, Tracey, and my younger son, Steve, always maintained optimism that I would recover. Joan, who had shared the ups and downs of my roller-coaster life in fifty-two years of marriage, girded herself for the battle. She was a veteran when it came to illness, and she accompanied me on each of my chemotherapy treatments. "I cope with the next illness by blocking," she remarked. "I just decide he will be fine and move on" by pushing it out of her mind. She has described herself as having "no attitude" rather than "a positive attitude." That was the most beneficial attitude I could have been exposed to. My family, my friends, and so many others who reached out by virtue of the simple fact that I represent them in the Senate, did not have to verbalize what was happening. Simply being there was enough for me to know that I was never alone in the struggle, and that I had a lot to live for.

6

The Best Therapy

FAR AND AWAY the best prize that life offers is the chance to work hard at work worth doing." So asserted Theodore Roosevelt.[1] My father had just missed the Roosevelt administration when he arrived in America, but he brought with him an immigrant work ethic that was indistinguishable from the Roosevelt credo. My father worked hard out of necessity to support his family. Unlike the Roosevelts, it was not a philosophical choice. "Tend to business, Arlen, tend to business," I could still hear him say to alleviate doubt as to whether I should stray from what needed to be done. His children saw him give selflessly to support his family through the Great Depression. He valued the formal education he missed in his life, and he instilled a love of learning and a curiosity about the world around us. Some of my first exposure to politics came as I heard my father discuss world affairs with a friend who regularly visited Sunday mornings. No one among us better embodied the two traits we honored most than my brother Morton. When he died, I insisted his headstone read: "Honest, Hard-working."[2] The work ethic lives on in my sons Shanin, one of the most highly regarded attorneys in Pennsylvania, and Steve, who worked harder in medical school than I have ever seen anyone work, with the possible exception of Morton himself.

I like to work. It makes me feel I am accomplishing something—a dynamic even more intense in government, where the good you can do is magnified and a wasted moment is that much more regrettable. As Senator Leahy said about me, "When he's working, he knows he's alive." That work also can be therapeutic in the face of adversity was demonstrated by Senator Biden just after he was first elected to the Senate in 1972 at the age of twenty-nine. The month before he started, his wife and children were in a tragic car accident that killed his wife and infant daughter and left his two sons badly injured. Joe was too devastated to start his Senate duties immediately, but by March of his first year in office, he started taking the train every day from Wilmington to Washington. Senator Bill Bradley, a star basketball player and colleague from 1979 to 1997, wrote:

[O]n one of his first days on the job he went into the senators' private dining room for lunch. When he got up to get a salad, the venerable and dour John McClellan of Arkansas summoned him: "Biden?"

"Yes, sir?"

"Lost your wife, huh?"

Biden bristled. The remark had the tone of "Lost the election, huh?"

"I think I know how you feel," said McClellan.

Biden didn't believe that the older senator had a clue about how he felt, but he held his tongue.

"Sit down, son," said McClellan, who then proceeded to share a part of his life with the young senator. "When I was thirty-six, my wife and I were driving back to Arkansas," McClellan said. "We got down in the Ozarks of Missouri, and suddenly she took sick. Within a few hours, she died. I had to raise three boys. It was difficult, but I did it. Twenty years later, I got a call from Aramco, in Saudi Arabia, where one of my sons was working. I was told he had been crushed to death on an oil rig and his body was on its way home. I went back to Little Rock and called another of my boys to ask him to join me and meet the plane that carried his brother's body. On the way to the airport, his motorcycle crashed, and he died. So there I was, with two dead boys arriving on the same day. So, son, I think I do understand. Now, let me give you this advice: work, work, work, work. That will pull you through." [3]

Senator Biden's tragedies are beyond anything I have ever endured, but in that context, no one could have said it better than Senator McClellan. His advice works just as well for an individual illness. Of that I am certain.

When Billy Tauzin told me of his experiences with cancer, I noted how similar they were to mine. He said that he marveled at my ability to continue work in the midst of the chemotherapy treatments, which were universally found to be disabling. When I told him that I insisted on staying on the job, he analogized it to his undertaking strenuous exercise, driving a bulldozer or tractor on his Louisiana ranch and disregarding his doctor's orders. He said that he thought he had to fight it through. And as I later fought the dual effects of cancer and chemotherapy while staying on the job, I knew exactly what he meant.

Senator Graham, whose mother died of Hodgkin's disease after a late-stage diagnosis in 1976, knew well "how devastating this illness can be, and how difficult the treatments are." As for how to respond to it, "it depends on who you are and what motivates you, but the key to these diseases is to not let them get you down. Have something to focus on, to work toward." In my case, he said he considered me "the type of person that lives for his work" and is driven by service in the Senate. The skills that allowed me "to become a political survivor—that determination and focused energy—were great skills to have to beat cancer." During the months that followed my diagnosis, he observed, "He came into our meeting room many times looking pretty weary, but mentally sharp." Lindsey was surprised and appreciative that I "stayed till everybody had a say, and never cut anyone short."

The Monday after my first chemotherapy treatment found me fatigued and achy, but it was fortunately the

Presidents Day holiday. I was determined to move ahead with scheduled appointments for the balance of the week. When I awoke the next morning, though, I felt like staying in bed. But I had a full day of events that had been scheduled weeks before, so I dragged myself to work. It was a tough day. First came a 9:00 A.M. news conference with the Black Clergy of Philadelphia and Senator Santorum. From my position on the Appropriations Committee, I had taken the lead in securing $4 million for minority job training to be administered by the Black Clergy. I did considerably better than other Republicans in Philadelphia with black voters, and I hoped to transfer some of my good will to my colleague for his reelection bid the following year.

I then pushed myself through another appointment—a visit to a West Philadelphia education project—before breaking for a short afternoon nap. That evening, I took Senator Santorum to an event with the Federation of Jewish Agencies. Here again, I hoped to urge support from a group where I was popular and he had less contact. The following day, I took the early train to Washington for a meeting with *The Washington Post* editorial board, a series of staff meetings, a haircut, and an afternoon nap in my hideaway. Not since the aftermath of my 1998 bypass had that sizable couch seemed so necessary. It was not the busiest of days for me, but I was exhausted enough that night to retire by 9:15 and sleep for almost eleven hours.

Requests had been mounting for interviews on the Judiciary Committee agenda and my physical condition. I held an hour-long news conference Thursday morning, February

24, to an overflow crowd in the Senate Radio/TV Gallery. Early on, a reporter's question got right to the point:

> [T]he medical problems you face now are going to be grueling. At a time when we're facing probably the toughest list the Judiciary Committee has had to face in some time—the judicial nominations and a possible Supreme Court battle—will your medical condition allow you to have the energy to do this job?[4]

After reminding the reporters of my Warren Commission work, Dr. Glick's diagnosis, and my squash regimen, I answered affirmatively: "I expect to be able to do the job. I always have." More convincing than this answer was the stamina I displayed in answering thirty-three questions in a news conference that lasted an hour. Many of those questions concerned an issue of great consequence to American government, perhaps the toughest in my twenty-five-year tenure—judicial nominations. In retrospect, I think the mounting pressure I felt and my exertions in connection with the issue of judicial nominations contributed to the stress of 2004. This would be a source of ongoing tension in 2005.

The week before my hour-long news conference, President Bush renominated twenty judicial nominees, ten of whom had been filibustered in 2004.[5] The development came as no surprise. *The New York Times* had reported back on Christmas Eve, a slow news day, that the renominations were forthcoming. In that same story, notwithstanding the shaky footing of my impending chairmanship, I challenged the president's announcement, saying, "I would have preferred to have some time in the 109th Congress to improve the climate to avoid judicial gridlocks and future filibusters . . . [so that] we might be able to approach this whole issue with some cooler perspective." Still, I continued, the president had acted within his prerogatives, so I added that I would "play the cards that were dealt" in trying to get his nominees considered.[6] It was the Senate's constitutional responsibility to confirm or reject judges, and the Judiciary Committee's responsibility to consider the nominations before they went to the full Senate.

The man who picked up the December gauntlet was the Judiciary Committee Democrat who led the fight against President Bush's judicial nominees based on ideology: Senator Chuck Schumer. The scrappy but sharp senator from New York was just finishing his first term when he responded to President Bush: "In this opening shot, the White House is making it clear that they are not interested in bipartisanship when it comes to nominating judges. This starts to poison the well when everyone on our side was hoping to make a new start."[7] The comment did not do justice to the potency of the Democratic filibuster or the polarization it created. The term "filibuster" evolved from the Dutch word for pirate, and while it has occasionally appeared in Senate history in the context of legislation (which Congress initiates and has the power to revise), it was virtually unheard-of as a tool to block judicial nominations (which the president initiates and the Senate merely gives its approval or disapproval). Whether in control or not, senators had long voted for qualified nominees of a president of an opposing party as a matter of deference. Now, they were not merely voting against such nominees, but casually employing the filibuster to prevent nominees with majority support from receiving a Senate vote at all.

The judge wars had been brewing for almost two decades. In 1987, after the Democrats gained control of the Senate, there was a slowdown in confirming President Ronald Reagan's nominees, and it continued during the presidency of George Bush the elder. The Democrats denied hearings to seven of President Reagan's nominees for circuit courts—which hear appeals from district courts before they reach the Supreme Court—and denied floor votes to two more. As a result, the confirmation rate for Reagan's circuit court nominees fell from 89 percent prior to the Democratic takeover to 65 percent afterward.

Republicans retaliated by refusing to confirm many of President Clinton's nominees after winning control of the Senate in 1994. Individual senators employed various maneuvers to block sixty of President Clinton's nominees. When it became clear that the Republican-controlled Senate would not allow the nominations to move forward, President Clinton withdrew twelve of those nominations and chose not to renominate sixteen. During that time, I urged my Republican colleagues on the Judiciary Committee to confirm well-qualified Democratic nominees, breaking ranks to vote for Marsha Berzon and Richard Paez to the Court of Appeals for the Ninth Circuit, H. Lee Sarokin for the Third Circuit, and Bill Lann Lee for assistant attorney general for the Justice Department's Civil Rights Division. This drew some criticism, but I had thoroughly reviewed their records and determined that they were qualified for the positions. I did not agree with these nominees on every issue, but I realized the importance of working toward solutions when the Senate is at an impasse on a nomination. My record allowed me to establish significant credibility with my Democratic colleagues when I became chairman.

When Democrats regained control of the Senate with Senator Jim Jeffords's defection in mid-2001—he voted with them after switching from Republican to independent—the new majority employed the filibuster to stop President Bush's nominees. After the 2002 elections, with control of the Senate returning to Republicans, the Democrats filibustered ten circuit court nominations, which was the most extensive use of the tactic in the nation's history. The 108th Congress saw a total of twenty cloture motions on ten nominations. All twenty failed. Three more circuit nominees were threatened with a filibuster, but never reached a cloture vote. Each move and countermove since Reagan's presidency had ratcheted up the ante until President Bush exercised his constitutional authority to make interim appointments, which he later abandoned in the face of a Democratic threat to shut down the Senate.

In the face of this impasse, Republicans developed a strategy they called the "constitutional option" because it was based on the interpretation that confirmations require only a majority of fifty-one senators under the Constitution. They argued that if the Framers had intended otherwise, they would have specified a supermajority or a two-thirds vote requirement, as they had for overriding the President's veto, ratifying treaties, or convicting on impeachment charges. A decade earlier, several Democratic senators who now supported the filibuster had made similar arguments against it.

The constitutional option was nicknamed the "nuclear option" by those who thought it would "blow up" the institution by eliminating the Senate's most unique attribute, unlimited debate. Implementation of the strategy called for bringing in the vice president, who presides over the Senate, to rule that only fifty-one senators were necessary to impose cloture or cut off debate so senators could vote. That ruling of the presiding officer would be sustained by a fifty-one-vote majority, which would make it final. While the issue between 2001 and 2004 involved only circuit court judges, it was anticipated that it could make the difference in determining the next vacancy on the nation's highest court.

Thus, between the filibuster and the constitutional or nuclear option, the Senate faced dual threats. One or more Supreme Court vacancies were expected in 2005, and that would carry the highest stakes. If a filibuster left an eight-person Court, the country could expect many four-to-four votes since the Court often decided cases with five-to-four votes. A Supreme Court tie vote would render the Court dysfunctional, leaving the decisions in effect among the twelve circuit courts, with divisions among them on the meaning of the law. A final decision would be suspended on many major issues. Yet if Republicans employed the constitutional or nuclear option, the Democrats threatened to retaliate by stopping the Senate agenda on all matters except national security and homeland defense. Thus the "nuclear" aspect of the option; it bore some resemblance to the MAD (mutual assured destruction) scenario during the age of the nuclear arms race between the United States and the Soviet Union.

This potential problem occupied the backdrop of my February 24 press conference far more than my illness. I used that opportunity, as I would many more, to criticize the excessive use of the filibuster and call for statesmanship to prevail on both sides. I should not have been surprised that my press conference was followed in the Senate Radio/TV Gallery by another with Senator Schumer, who capitalized on the moment to launch his next political volley. After telling the assembled reporters he was "so delighted that" I was "feisty and fighting and thoughtful," he announced the latest letter he had sent the White House in his effort to increase Democratic influence over judicial nominations. I was unaware of the letter, designed to pressure me to meet with the president about judicial nomina-

At the Annenberg Public Policy Center in Philadelphia during my formal campaign announcement tour in January 2004. Campaigning was the most fun when family members joined me. From left to right, my daughter-in-law, Tracey Specter, holds Hatti, the youngest of my four granddaughters; Lilli hugs her grandfather; Perri peeks through the microphones; my wife, Joan, stands to my right; and Silvi looks on from the far right. *(Author's collection)*

Between campaign stops and official events, a day of campaigning in 2004 often included a dozen or more stops. Here I am on the campaign trail talking to workers. *(Author's collection)*

The night of the primary election, April 27, 2004, saw a narrow victory after an evening that was as suspenseful as the campaign had been. Among the crowd of family and friends are Joan and Silvi at the podium to the left and Tracey with my son, Shanin, to the right. Standing behind Joan is my chief of staff, Carey Lackman. *(Author's collection)*

The joy of the primary victory was followed by the tragic death of Carey Lackman less than three months later after her struggle with breast cancer. A personable, brilliant, and studious leader who was a mentor for the young staff, Carey posed with Mayor Rudolph Giuliani and me in April 2003. *(Ivan J. Papurt)*

Joan and I took this picture with Paula Kline and her husband, Tom, at Paula's fiftieth birthday party in 2000. A bright, energetic, and spunky lady, Paula was a champion of theater and literature and a devoted mother of two. The Klines have long been close friends of the Specters, and her death from breast cancer shortly after my 2004 general election victory was a devastating loss for our family. *(Tom Kline)*

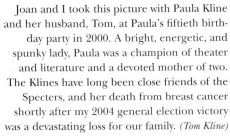

On January 6, 2006, before the Hodgkin's diagnosis, I wielded the gavel at the confirmation hearing of Attorney General Alberto Gonzales after waiting twenty-four years to become chairman of the Senate Judiciary Committee. *(Jim Bourg/Reuters/Corbis)*

Notwithstanding my efforts to keep a stiff upper lip at the February 24 news conference, my face in this photo depicts the pall and overhang of Hodgkin's. *(Jason Reed/Reuters/ Newscom)*

Dr. John Glick has an extraordinary reputation as one of America's preeminent oncologists. The consummate professional, he showed himself equal to his reputation when he treated me during my struggle with Hodgkin's. *(John Glick)*

I received my chemotherapy treatments in this chair and would look through this window during the process, admiring the skyline of my beloved city and occasionally reminiscing about the past. *(Carrie Stricker)*

This photo was taken on March 8, 2005, during a meeting in the White House with President Bush and Vice President Cheney on Social Security reform. Sitting next to me on the couch (left to right) are Sen. Kit Bond, Sen. Susan Collins, and Sen. John McCain. At this point, I am beginning to lose hair from my treatments. *(White House photo by Eric Draper)*

On April 5, 2005, Attorney General Alberto Gonzales and FBI Director Robert Mueller confer with Sen. Pat Leahy and me before the start of a Judiciary Committee hearing on the renewal of the Patriot Act. My hair loss by this time has become more stark. *(Getty Images)*

The cameras capture me up close at a news conference on the rights of blue-collar workers held on April 19, 2005. *(Getty Images)*

I was nearing total baldness when I met with Katie Couric on May 9, 2005, to tape a *Today Show* interview. *(Author's collection)*

Feeling the cumulative, heavy effects nearing the end of my chemotherapy treatment on July 12, 2005, I visited Vice President Cheney in his office just off the Senate floor, bald, pale, and tired—referring to myself, not the Vice President. However, I was able to sit up straight in my chair. *(White House photo by David Bohrer)*

On July 18, 2005, I had just come from meeting Karl Rove and Harriet Miers at the White House reviewing the president's short list for Justice O'Connor's vacancy on the Supreme Court when I pitched one inning and hit a grounder to third in the annual Specter/Santorum softball game. An ABC News profile of me featured my performance on the field. *(ABC News)*

On July 20, 2005, the day after his nomination to the Supreme Court was announced, John Roberts met with me privately in my Senate hideaway. During the media frenzy that day, I told reporters that I planned on holding fair, detailed hearings and that I hoped people would keep the rhetoric to a minimum and wait for Judge Roberts to be heard. *(Author's collection)*

On July 21, 2005, the day before my last chemotherapy treatment, I attended a meeting with President Bush in the family quarters of the White House to discuss the Roberts nomination. His body language and facial expression suggest that, considering my bald head and pale face, he doubts whether I'm going to make it. *(White House photo by Eric Draper)*

The July 21 meeting included President Bush, Vice President Cheney, and White House staff members who handled the nomination. Facing the president on the couch in the foreground are (left to right) Senate Republican Whip Mitch McConnell and chief of staff Andy Card. Sitting next to me on the couch toward the back is Majority Leader Bill Frist. Sitting third from right among the White House officials is White House Counsel Harriet Miers.
(White House photo by Eric Draper)

On August 17, 2005, I traveled to Venezuela to meet President Hugo Chavez and broker a deal on drug interdiction with his minister of the interior and our U.S. ambassador. *(Author's collection)*

During my illness, I remained determined to maintain my regular squash schedule, but at the height of my chemotherapy, I had to cut my usual five or six games to two or three. It did not matter whether I was at home or abroad. Here I am on a squash court with a partner during my August 2005 Latin American trip. *(Author's collection)*

On September 14, 2005, the front page of *The New York Times* captured some of the intensity of my opening thirty minutes of questioning of the to-be chief justice at the beginning of the confirmation hearing the day before.

On October 3, 2005, Senator Frist and I met with Harriet Miers after the president's announcement that morning of her nomination to the Supreme Court. At this point, my hair is visibly growing back. *(Getty Images)*

On December 20, 2005, Senator Frist and I met with the Senate Republican Policy Committee in the Capitol to discuss the Senate's logjam on the reauthorization of the Patriot Act. My once curly hair grew back almost entirely straight, with a little wave in the front. *(Getty Images)*

A political cartoon by Chip Bok lampooned the nomination hearings for Samuel Alito with a depiction of Sen. Ted Kennedy and me fighting. Sen. Joe Biden on the right has his arm raised in the air as if still in mid-speech. Sen. Orrin Hatch sits with a smile on the left while Sen. Pat Leahy asks the nominee, "This respect of yours for the legislative branch, judge...Where's that come from?" *(By permission of Chip Bok and Creators Syndicate, Inc.)*

When Justice Alito came into my office on January 26, 2006, after his confirmation hearing, my hair was back and I was relaxed. I was smiling, although not as broadly and as happily as he had been while making his way across the street after surviving the rugged hearing at the Supreme Court—visible through the window. *(Author's collection)*

Judge Edward Becker, my friend of over fifty years, did not allow prostate cancer to keep him from applying his immense intelligence, character, and work ethic to mediating the asbestos issue. Here he testifies before the Judiciary Committee on the qualifications of his colleague on the Third Circuit, Samuel Alito, four months before his death on May 19, 2006. *(Congressional Quarterly/Getty Images)*

Back to my normal squash schedule, I continue to play virtually daily. Here I play in 2007 with Daniel Fisher, age 26, who works on my Judiciary Committee staff. *(Author's collection)*

Marrying the right person can be a profound benefit to your health. I might not have made it without Joan vigilantly at my side during all my medical challenges.
(Tracey Specter)

Joan and I join our sons Shanin (left) and Steve (right) for a casual moment in 2006. Shanin is a successful Philadelphia attorney. Steve, a Ph.D. in nutrition and an M.D., is currently in residency in California. Their counsel to me over the years has been invaluable, in battles political as well as medical.
(Tracey Specter)

Here I am at the August 2006 unveiling of a motorbike at a women's center in Nepal. Seeing the grin on my face, which apparently resembled my expression on election night 2004, the staffer who snapped my picture thought to himself, It's official: We're back!
(Chris Bradish)

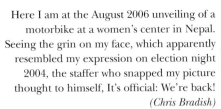

tions, prior to Senator Schumer's announcement to the press. In *The Washington Post*'s words, "Schumer repaid Specter's candor with a stunt."[8]

That afternoon, I headed back to Philadelphia for a dinner meeting and proceeded to New York early the next morning for a meeting with *The New York Times* editorial board. I then returned to Philadelphia that afternoon for follow-up medical tests. That turned out to be a typical week, to be followed by many others like it. Since I thought the best therapy for the fatigue and debilitating chemotherapy treatments was a heavy work schedule, I felt lucky to have so much on my shoulders (or so at least I thought).

I appeared on CNN's *Late Edition* the Sunday after my return to work. Wolf Blitzer wasted no time to ask the health question: "A lot of us were very, very concerned when we got word a couple weeks or so ago that you now have Hodgkin's disease. . . . That can be quite debilitating, can't it?" Wolf sounded genuinely concerned. I responded that I still could do my job:

I'm very optimistic generally, Wolf. I think, if you approach these problems with a positive attitude and try to explore all the alternatives on the judicial situation, on asbestos reform, on a lot of issues that I have faced— and I did beat a brain tumor, beat it twice, bypass surgery, a lot of tough political opponents. And I've got a lot of energy, Wolf. I had a news conference that lasted almost an hour in Washington last Thursday; I answered a lot of questions. And watch me, Wolf. Watch me.[9]

Although my appearance had not changed at that time, Blitzer's focus was on my health. The questions he raised would recur in many interviews: What stage was the cancer? How debilitating could it be? How would I be able to carry out my Senate duties? I kept a stiff upper lip and meant every word when I sent my message to other cancer patients to maintain a positive attitude.

Like it or not, my appearance inevitably would become a message unto itself. During the month of March, as the Judiciary Committee began to tackle confirmation of the filibustered judges and other nominees, I lost most of my hair and grew pale and drawn. As my hair disappeared, I received many suggestions on what I should do about my growing baldness. Some said I should shave my head and become a sex symbol. I rejected that on two counts: I did not want to do that, and it would not work. Others suggested wearing a baseball cap or a wig. I confess I considered the baseball cap option initially. I had worn one for several days after my brain surgery in 1993. That was different, however; I had a large, ugly scar at the time.

This time I would allow nature to take its course and do all I could to ignore it, even if others showed an inversely proportional awareness of my appearance. I would keep to my normal routine, which meant not only work, but also my regular trips to the Senate barber. I asked Tony Calabro, who cut my hair for eighteen years, simply to even things out as different parts of my hair grew at an irregular length. My hair entirely disappeared by June. Except for a stretch of a couple of months when there was simply nothing to cut, I kept my barbershop appointments even when in retrospect it probably was absurd to tend to such a meager amount of fuzz. I once amused Dr. Glick's staff by walking in for a chemotherapy treatment wearing a cowboy hat, but I had put it on because it was raining hard that day.

In early March I called my Pennsylvania staff to Washington so that I could fill everyone in on my medical situation. After speaking with everyone collectively, I took aside Andy Wallace, executive director for my northeastern Pennsylvania offices, for his insight as a cancer survivor. Andy, age fifty-two, had overcome non-Hodgkin's lymphoma seven years earlier and prostate cancer two years earlier. He gently advised me to step back from work, but I told him that's just not the way it would be. There was a lot to be done. I know Andy understood. Although he had nothing more to prove after all he had endured, his non-Hodgkin's lymphoma would return in May—this time more aggressively than before—bringing him back to chemotherapy in none other than Dr. Glick's office. He went bald, and some complimented him on the assumption he had shaved his head out of sympathy. Yet even that ordeal would not get the better of him. Andy continues to serve as my northeastern Pennsylvania director.

I found in Andy a role model for how to deal with disease even before his non-Hodgkin's recurred, and I was fortunate to have many models such as Carey Lackman and Paula Kline, as well as Judge Becker. Ed and I called each other the "chemo kids," and Ed had a knack for stating matter-of-factly the modern reality of living with cancer: "The bottom line is, you can be under chemotherapy and work seven days a week. You get some fatigue. You take a nap and work through it. The last couple of years have been the most productive I've ever had in my life."[10] Another friend with a similar situation was Herb Barness, who served as my campaign organization's finance chairman for many years. Herb died in 1998 after struggling with non-Hodgkin's lymphoma for more than seven years, but he left his friends with memories of a wonderful, warm man who never allowed his illness to diminish his cheerfulness. When asked how he felt, he would often reply, "Great." As he would say, "Every day's a good day. Some are better than others." Herb drew a distinction between having a disease and being sick, and he rarely if ever missed a day of work. His daughter Lynda, who worked in my district office during the 1980s, was diagnosed with breast cancer a few years after her father died, and she carried his positive attitude with her. Herb taught her that such an attitude is a gift to those around us.

I could never outdo Herb's cheerfulness, but I did keep my eye on the half-full part of the glass. When my colleagues asked, I was always doing okay, which was true. At worst, I would add, "I could do better," but I felt remarkably on top of my game even at my lowest ebb. During the course of the treatment and afterward, I never felt my concentration or judgment was impaired. As I told *The Philadelphia Inquirer,* "When you're working, you're thinking about your work, which is, I think, a healthy thing to do . . . I call it extra-special therapy."[11] As I pointed out earlier, Shanin had suggested that the cumulative effect of the chemotherapy would make the continuing treatments more troublesome, and that prospect worried me. Fortunately, however, that would not be the case, or at least did not seem to be the case. Shanin and others maintain that I did get progressively worse. If I did not notice the regression, it was due to my own bodily adjustment. Dr. Glick made the process that much easier by being there for me. As I began treatments, he called me almost every day, and when I would call him, three out of four or four out of five times, he would pick up instantly with his familiar salutation, "Dr. Glick." Over the course of our conversations, we have become good friends.

I received a wonderful piece of news after enduring four treatments over eight weeks. On April 8, Dr. Glick administered a PET scan that turned out negative, indicating that there was no metabolically active Hodgkin's disease. A simultaneous CT scan showed extensive improvement from the February 16 test, with relatively little Hodgkin's disease in the nodes. My prognosis became more favorable, and the doctor decided my treatments would end after twelve rather than sixteen rounds. The CT scans and PET scans would continue every several months, but matters were on the right track. As for Dr. Glick, I could not be more impressed with the thoroughness of his work. He would examine me under the arms to detect problems in the lymph nodes, listen to my heart, listen to the rest of my chest, lie me down, and lift me over. He was thorough to the nth degree. I like to say he practices medicine the way I try to practice senatoring. From his rich experience, Dr. Glick almost always had answers to my questions. One exception was when I complained to him that my libido was lagging; he had no answer for that, except to remark that that was normal. He might have added that was not the worst affliction a guy could suffer. All things considered, my doctor made it that much easier for me not to focus too much on my illness.

That said, my immediate battle had been—and remained—the cancer treatments more than the cancer itself. From the time I started treatment in February until about six weeks after my last cocktail on July 22, I felt well only when heavily engaged in work, which gave me less time to dwell on how lousy I felt. Long nights of sleep and frequent naps were indispensable. Unless the Senate had an evening session, I was in bed weekdays by 8:30 to get nine hours before my internal wake-up alarm got me up at 5:30 for my daily squash game. I often did not feel like getting up. It required an effort to push myself out of bed and onto the squash court.[12] I was still determined to maintain my regular squash schedule, but at the height of my chemotherapy, I had to cut my usual five or six games to two or three. On one occasion, I had to find a deserted spot in the locker room to give myself my Neulasta injection, which Evan Kelly, my partner that day, found unsettling.

My warm-up exercises also had to be reduced. I cut my pregame leg stretches in half, from twelve to six, to conserve my energy for the match itself. In the shower, I found I couldn't lift my legs or bend over sufficiently to wash my feet, but I persevered with a little less soap and a lot more water on some parts of my body.

Of course, the mind demands exercise as much as the body. Andy Gleason, a Johnstown, Pennsylvania, resident over a hundred years old recently told me, "Arlen, when you get to be ninety, it's good to think about things you've done. You've got to keep your mind active." Before starting Senate business every morning, I read three newspapers: I scoured every line of the national and international news in *The New York Times.* I read *The Washington Post* to keep up with the high school, as I sometimes call the Congress. I included *The Philadelphia Inquirer* to follow Pennsylvania news. I also kept with me a decent stock of outside reading, including the acclaimed tome by Robert Caro, *Master of the Senate,* a study of Lyndon B. Johnson and the very different Senate of his day. My staff additionally prepared me a daily diet of news clips.

President Bush is known to put great value in self-discipline, and he said he was intrigued by my management of workload, exercise, chemo, and regular naps as a matter of self-discipline. I napped every day in my hideaway for thirty to forty minutes, with many two-nap days and an occasional three-nap day. During my lunch break, I would grab a salad or soup and retreat to my hideaway for a siesta until the bells rang for a vote, which required my presence on the Senate floor. By juggling my schedule, I found more nap time between hearings, meetings, and constituent calls. Every Monday morning, I would be driven to work, leaving my home at 7:00 A.M. and arriving in Washington at about 10:00 A.M. The drive, although forty-five minutes longer than Amtrak, was less tiring and kept me off the drafty station platforms and away from potentially contagious colds or viruses from fellow passengers. Although I did not realize it at the time, riding with me was not easy during that period, because I kept the heat up in the car to combat my coldness, and other passengers would lower their windows. I would sleep all the way and then go directly to my hideaway for another nap. I also maintained my habit of going to the steam room in the Senate gym for a massage between 5:45 and 6:15 P.M., frequently after the last vote of the day. When I arrived at my Georgetown condo after work, I would make myself a martini before retiring for the evening. Since becoming chairman of the Judiciary Committee, I scheduled regular dinner meetings at my condo with committee staff to coordinate our work and share some light moments. The light moments were not as light during my illness, because I was as prone in my chronic chilliness to overheat my condo as I was my car.

The Sundays following my Friday treatments were especially tough. My most frequent squash partner at the time, Evan Kelly, recalls with sadness those trips to the squash court near the Bellevue-Stratford Hotel, where I typically played the game on weekends. Our normal morning gabbing gave way to periods of several minutes where I sat staring at the lockers, trying to collect my strength. On a few such occasions, I skipped squash and slept on an unused massage table with a jacket placed over me because I was cold. If I did not have the energy for both squash and the Phillies, I chose the baseball game. I found going to sporting events, musicals, and movies to be other pleasant weekend diversions, and I listened often to my favorite music—largely standards from the big band era, and especially the music of the greatest entertainer who ever lived, Frank Sinatra. My principal diversions from Hodgkin's, however, remained work, squash, and family—which are never entirely separate. I like to see my grandchildren at least once on weekends when I can, and we occasionally play squash. Silvi was the only one old enough to play formal squash games. Lilli and Hatti are now becoming pretty good too.

Joan is a very energetic and active person who can be challenging to follow. She has long been better read than I on the subject of health, and she was a believer in alternative, herbal, and holistic treatments long before I was diagnosed with Hodgkin's. I am skeptical of some of these treatments, but always respectful and open to trying them. Some of these options were off the table, because Dr. Glick feared that herbs and certain vitamins might interfere with chemotherapy. Left to my own devices, I took to eating foods like hot dogs, pizza, and cheeseburgers, which are not particularly healthy. This made Joan uncomfortable, but she was aware of

Dr. Glick's recommendation of high-calorie, high-protein foods. Everyone tolerated my nightly martinis.

Eating was a challenge as my treatments progressed, especially on weekends following chemo. There was little I could taste, notwithstanding a solicitous staff who did their best. In the early mornings following squash, my driver, David Debruyn, and Evan Kelly would get me a danish, which I relished because it was so sweet. That was the closest I typically had to breakfast. Later in the day, I would eat spicy foods or down the energy drink Boost, which had the delightful taste of a chocolate milk shake. It somewhat reminded me of a "smooth"—a fifteen-cent black-and-white milk shake I used to get at the Russell Drug Store back in high school. Alison Cooper arranged with the chefs in the Senate dining room to prepare for me a menu featuring the popular Dean Ornish diet, but I never felt up to requesting it. Fortunately, I still could enjoy periodic dinners at the Prime Rib with staff from my campaign organization. I came to detest foods with strong smells and even drinking straight water. My drink of choice became Gatorade, which I brought everywhere with me—every variety of the drink but the purple, which turned my mouth that color. For my condition, Dr. Glick noted that the electrolytes in the drink made it preferable to water.

Not surprisingly, my change of appetite brought a loss of weight. With a height of five feet, ten inches, I had been nearly 179 pounds about a week before the 2004 general election, and my weight dropped almost 16 pounds to a low of 163 on July 5, 2005. The lines on my face became more pronounced as I grew gaunt. I remarked that I looked like Sam Rayburn, the legendary Speaker of the House, shortly before he died. My hair and eyebrows entirely disappeared, and my voice became somewhat faded. Senator Harkin once took me by the arm and was shocked to discover "there was just nothing there." Other problems persisted. I would nearly lose my balance on occasion. Although I never fell, my equilibrium was shaky for months. Similarly, my nose ran for months, and my eyes tear to this day. Besides Gatorade, boxes of tissues were always at my side. I developed mouth sores and found regular toothpaste burned my mouth. A special mild brand of toothpaste, Biotene, solved that problem. The chemo cocktails caused constipation, so Dr. Glick recommended a gentle laxative, Senokot, to redress that problem.

The newspapers had their own take on my changing appearance. The *Pittsburgh Post-Gazette* wrote on June 19, "His wavy reddish hair is gone, his once full cheeks have hollowed, his suits hang on his angular frame . . . he is visibly weaker." Six days later, the *Los Angeles Times* agreed: "The skin is ashen and hangs from the corners of his mouth. The eyes are rimmed with red . . . he no longer recognizes the face that greets him in the bathroom mirror." My old friend, John Baer, could not put a good face on my appearance when he wrote a May 4 *Philadelphia Daily News* column about me: "[T]he hair loss (almost none is left) due to chemotherapy makes him look thinner and, well, sickly." But Baer also noted that I had beaten the odds many times in the past and remarked, "I've never counted him out. And I don't now."[13] That was reassuring.

The person who may have observed me most closely during my bout with Hodgkin's was Chris Picaut, chief of staff to the attending physician to the Capitol. He saw me enter the office dozens of times and commented about watching me on C-SPAN2, which covers Senate proceedings on the floor as well as committee hearings. After seeing me in the doctor's office, knowing I was feeling terrible, he was struck at how he would then observe me "going into a committee hearing or walking onto the Senate floor, battling with other senators, and carrying on my work as if I was just fine." I was proud when Chris complimented my studious approach to medical issues, remarking that I discussed them with the doctors almost on their level. After watching me barrage Dr. John Eisold, the attending physician, with questions from my own medical research, he commented, "It's almost like he's gone through a board again." Jean Larsen, the nurse in that office who usually took care of me, did a tremendous job besides being fun to speak with. She was one of the people I knew who told me my bald look was stylish. She asked me early one week, not long after my diagnosis, "Did you have a chance to relax, to get away from the stress this weekend?"

I replied, "Jean, I don't have stress. I'm a carrier." I adapted this quip from a conversation I once had with Penn State football coach Joe Paterno. The coach had coal-black hair that was unusual for his age, and he was accompanied to a 1983 Judiciary Committee hearing by two younger, gray-haired assistant coaches. After the hearing, I jokingly asked Paterno, "Coach, how come your hair is so black and your younger assistants are gray?"

"Well, Senator," he replied, "it's like it was with Vince Lombardi. Everybody around him had ulcers; but not Vince. He was asked a similar question—why everyone around had ulcers, but not him. 'It's simple,' Lombardi explained, 'I'm a carrier.' Same thing with me, Senator. I'm a carrier."[14]

I kept a log of how I felt every day through my chemotherapy treatments and some time thereafter, assigning a letter grade between A and F to each day. This helped me project how I would feel going forward, and it was reassuring to see improvement follow every decline. In the end, the grades were all over the A-to-D range, usually higher rather than lower, but because I was able to go to work regardless of how lousy I felt, the grades were passing. Only one weekday earned an F: Thursday, June 30. That was an excruciatingly difficult day on which I arose at 6:00, missed squash, and attended a Judiciary markup, numerous meetings, and a party, with two votes scheduled at night—one on CAFTA, a Central American trade agreement, and one on an energy bill. I made it to the first vote, but just could not stay for the second. Although I put in a 16½-hour day (albeit with interspersed naps), I assigned it an F because that was the only time in my Senate career I ever went home at night without going to a scheduled vote.

People often would do a double take when they saw me, whether in person or on television. Is that Arlen? some remarked they would think in disbelief as they saw me. My friend Peter Hearn, who had seen at least fifteen people he knew endure cancer, observed that "Arlen with no hair was as startling a change in the appearance of somebody as I've ever seen." Andy Wallace would speak of how many friends did not recognize him. He would often feel like a stranger in familiar settings, from a hometown street to his office. The first time I visited my grandchildren with most of my hair missing, nine-year-old Perri and four-year-old Hatti found the sight "scary" and thought I looked older. Lilli asked, "Arlen, what happened to your hair?" I explained that I took this medicine that caused my hair to fall out. "It kind of felt like it was somebody else and not him the first time I saw him," she later commented. "He looked like a stranger." But as time went by, she added, "I got used to it."

I was really shocked on one occasion in June, while I attended a Philadelphia 76ers basketball game. Governor Rendell walked right by me twice, and both times, my friend of over thirty years did not recognize me attempting to say hi to him.

The Judiciary Committee was considering legislation on "identity theft" at the time my appearance was changing, and I joked that when I looked in the mirror, I felt I was a victim of that very crime. My colleague from Montana, Senator Conrad Burns, lightened things up in his wisecracky style: "I got an e-mail from a constituent. Likes you better bald. Doesn't like you either way, but likes you better bald."

When I was with Senator Leahy, who is completely bald except for a ring of hair around the edges, I quipped that I could be identified as the fellow with the red tie. "The only drawback," Pat told me, "is you get your hair back; I don't."

"Pat," I replied, "you don't want to go through what I went through to get your hair back." I had a hard time watching myself, partly because I knew so many people were watching me so intently.

Up close, many I encountered seemed more likely to focus on my balding head than on making eye contact. Even television viewers would notice my forehead glistening as I exerted myself. My Senate colleagues were sympathetic, but many seemed to have a hard time watching my deterioration. I sensed they wondered whether my assertions that I would recover were a form of "whistling Dixie," putting the best face on a dire situation. Although the medical realities of the twenty-first century are otherwise, people still tend to equate baldness from cancer treatment with impending death. When I would walk into the well of the Senate, my colleagues would look at me and squint their eyes as if to say, "This guy ain't gonna make it."

The same thought occurred to a prospective Judiciary Committee staffer while I interviewed him in late March. He associated my appearance with his father's during treatments for a malignant and ultimately fatal brain tumor, which he suffered at the same time I had my benign tumor. Yet I had no problem hiring him and others who saw that our operation was going in full force. There was a comparable effect in my family. My Aunt Rose told me over the phone from Wichita, "I have strength just hearing you." Actions and words can go a long way even when you look like hell.

At least among domestic issues, the impending debate over judges was preeminent. There was an open question, not decided to this day, as to whether fifty-one of the fifty-five Republican senators would vote to sustain the constitutional/nuclear option. While all fifty-five opposed the Democrats' use of the filibuster, some were unwilling to change a fundamental Senate rule in order to confirm circuit court judges. I sought to diffuse the judicial impasse and avoid a vote on the constitutional/nuclear option by circulating memoranda designed to persuade Democrats to confirm several nominees. I scheduled the first hearing on March 1 for William Myers, a Ninth Circuit nominee who was only two votes short of the sixty needed to end his filibuster. Nothing worked. As positions hardened in the first four months of the 109th Congress, Senator Frist scheduled repeated cloture votes on several nominees without success.

Between March and May, the confrontation was reaching its apparent climax as the Judiciary Committee moved judicial nominee after nominee through hearings and markups to the full Senate. I still wanted to break the filibuster and see a meeting of the minds to avoid the confrontation, which meant appealing to my colleagues' statesmanship. Even on days when I felt my worst, I would go to the Senate floor to urge my colleagues to shed the straitjacket of party loyalty. "On these critical issues with these cataclysmic consequences," I stated on April 21—a day I graded a D in my personal log—"I urge my colleagues on both sides of the aisle to study the issues and to vote their consciences independent of party dictation." I had heard in the cloakrooms and corridors that there would not be forty-one Democratic votes for filibustering or fifty-one Republican votes for the constitutional/nuclear option if senators would independently vote their consciences instead of the party line.

On the Senate floor, I pressed the issue:

I have had many conversations with my Democrat colleagues about the filibuster of judicial nominees. Many of them have told me that they do not personally believe it is a good idea to filibuster President Bush's judicial nominees. They believe that this unprecedented use of the filibuster does damage to this institution and to the prerogatives of the President. Yet despite their concerns, they gave in to party loyalty and voted repeatedly to filibuster Federal judges in the last Congress.

Likewise, there are many Republicans in this body who question the wisdom of the constitutional or nuclear option. They recognize that such a step would be a serious blow to the rights of the minority that have always distinguished this body from the House of Representatives. Knowing that the Senate is a body that depends upon collegiality and compromise to pass even the smallest resolution, they worry that the rule change will impair the ability of this institution to function.[15]

Historically, heroic senators renowned as "profiles in courage," the title of John F. Kennedy's Pulitzer Prize–winning book, had protected and preserved the critical constitutional doctrine of separation of powers. In 1805, the Senate refused to convict Supreme Court Justice Samuel Chase on politically motivated impeachment charges, which saved the independence of the federal judiciary. In 1868, the Senate refused to convict President Andrew Johnson on impeachment charges by a single vote, which saved the power of the presidency. I tried to invoke such examples in making my plea from the floor:

> The lessons of our best days as a nation should serve as a model today for Senators to vote their consciences on the confirmation of judges and on the constitutional/nuclear option.
>
> If we fail, then I fear this Senate will descend the staircase of political gamesmanship and division. But if we succeed, our Senate will regain its place as the world's preeminent deliberative body.[16]

A shifting coalition of fifteen to twenty senators, fairly evenly divided between Republicans and Democrats, started meeting to discuss a way out of the impasse. In one floor statement, I analogized the changing compositions of the meetings, with different members coming in and out, to "a floating crap game." On two occasions, May 17 and 19, I joined the meetings. On May 17, Senators Bill Frist and Harry Reid attended, giving the implicit blessing of the party leaders to the effort of the group to find a way out. It was curious that the leaders were aiding and abetting the coup d'etat. Neither leader was willing explicitly and publicly to abandon his advocacy for filibustering or the constitutional option. Senator Frist was being egged on by the far right to ram the rule change down the Democrats' throats. Senator Reid was similarly being pressed by the far left to filibuster forever.

Eventually, a so-called Gang of Fourteen was formed by seven Republicans and seven Democrats.[17] They informally agreed to confirm three nominees and reject two. They had the votes to control the process. They adopted a policy not to filibuster in the future in the absence of "extraordinary circumstances," a term left deliberately vague. The key ingredient in this grand compromise was the uncertainty as to how the vote on the constitutional/nuclear option would come out. The speculation was that there would be a one-vote margin, and some said the uncertain vote was mine. But I thought it was important not to join the Gang so that I could retain a neutral position as chairman in mediating controversies over judges certain to arise in the Judiciary Committee. Sheryl Gay Stolberg of *The New York Times* wrote a story speculating on my vote on May 23, with publication due the next day, when the critical vote was scheduled.

The story was never published, because the Gang of Fourteen made a deal on Monday evening, May 23. That was a D-day for me, and I had gone to bed at 7:30 P.M. not knowing of the deal. I had carefully prepared a floor statement on my position on the anticipated vote, which I did not have to make and have never disclosed. When I awakened at 5:30 A.M. and heard the news at 6:00 on National Public Radio, I was enormously relieved to have personally dodged a bullet without announcing my judgment, but I was even more relieved for the Senate, which had dodged a potential nuclear bomb. Healthwise, May 24 was a somewhat better C–/D+ day for me, and the grades would continue to rise until falling again in early June. What if the filibuster fight returned during a Supreme Court confirmation? one reporter asked me. "I'll jump off that bridge when I come to it," I replied.[18]

Meanwhile, most of the previously filibustered circuit court nominees ended up being confirmed over the next several weeks. During one of those debates, Senator John Sununu walked by three of my counsels who handled nominations, all of whom happened to be bald and sitting together in the well of the Senate. He pointed at them and asked with a smile, "What's the deal, guys?"

After they identified themselves as Specter staffers, one of them jokingly replied, "Solidarity." Unaware that their baldness had well preceded my Hodgkin's diagnosis, Sununu was so moved by the apparent show of sympathy that he went nearly bald himself. Only the entreaties of his children prevented him from going 100 percent bald. After shaving his head, he pulled aside David Brog in a hallway one day to tell him, "Look what I did. I was so touched by what your staff did that I decided to do it too." The senator by that time was unrecognizable enough that David mistook him for a tourist—a tourist under an obvious misimpression about the staff. Senator Sununu was amused later to learn the full story and invited the bald staffers to his office for a group photo, which he would inscribe "Bald is beautiful!" and "My inspiration!"

With no rest for the weary, the key markup of the asbestos bill occurred on Thursday, May 26, less than three days after the Gang of Fourteen announcement. There the committee would make final amendments to the bill before (hopefully) reporting it to the floor. That was a particularly tough day for me, occurring as it did in the middle of my chemo treatments. My regular 6:30 A.M. squash match was cut short because I was winded after only two games. The markup session ended up lasting five hours (9:30 A.M. to 2:30 P.M.) without a lunch break for me. The chemotherapy had caused my sinuses to drip and my eyes to water even more that day than usual. I had ample amounts of Gatorade with me to keep up my fluids and Kleenex to keep my runny nose and watering eyes dry. It takes ten senators out of the eighteen members of the committee to be present to make a quorum to vote on amendments. Over the course of the long sessions, senators were difficult to track as they came and went in no discernible order. I was the only one present all day. I left the hearing room briefly at one point to go to a nearby room where some committee members were eating in order to bring them back to the markup.

The many amendments offered by Senator Biden were particularly contentious. He is noted for speaking at length, often passionately and occasionally over the top. His excessive verbosity got him into trouble frequently during his political career. Shortly after Senator Barack Obama's announcement for the presidency in 2007, Biden called Obama "the first mainstream African-American" presidential candidate "who is articulate and bright and clean and a nice-looking guy."[19] This statement was widely criticized, in large part for the implicit insults to prior African-American presidential candidates such as Shirley Chisholm, Jesse Jackson, Carol Moseley Braun, and Al Sharpton. Knowing Joe as I did, I was sure he had not intended to disparage anyone, but his remark got a difficult campaign off to a very rough start.

During the markup of the asbestos bill, Joe was intense and antagonistic. Some trial lawyers were ardent opponents of the asbestos bill, and the senator tended to be closely allied with that constituency. Battling Joe Biden that day was tough, but my most difficult fight was against the clock. Regarding his arguments, I told my colleague relatively early in the markup, "There are very compelling responses to all of those arguments, and it is difficult not to respond, but I'm fighting the clock more than I'm fighting these amendments." I knew how the votes would come out: The amendments would be rejected. I just did not know when he would stop talking and allow the votes to occur. I simply had to finish all pending amendments, or we would be back two weeks later following the Memorial Day recess, having to start all over again with a new batch of amendments.

I had learned the applicable lesson watching Senator Howard Baker, then majority leader, manage a tax bill in

1982. He sometimes kept the Senate in session all night to finish the legislation, because as he said, "Amendments, like mushrooms, grow overnight," and there would be more in the morning if he did not finish. It was an adage I never forgot.

Senator Biden would argue his amendments frequently in a diatribe. He was intense, antagonistic, and surly, and his behavior that day went beyond anything I had ever seen from him. Frankly, it was insulting. He shouted at one point in reference to an amendment he was offering to exclude certain asbestos settlements from the bill's coverage: "This is on the greed side. This is on the greed side. This is outrageous, absolutely, totally outrageous. My amendment I'll introduce and let you vote against it, and I can't believe this." Joe raised his voice to a louder volume than anyone on the committee ever did in the 109th Congress as his prospects for success diminished. At one point, even fellow Democrat Pat Leahy entered the following dialogue with Joe:[20]

LEAHY: Mr. Chairman, if I might just for a moment, I've heard what's been said—actually, I couldn't help but hear it.

BIDEN: I'm glad you're listening.

LEAHY: I have in my back yard at home a very nice pistol range where I love . . . to use any one of the dozen or so handguns that I have for target shooting, but I wear ear protection, substantial ear protection. And I must admit, today, I almost wish I had it.

BIDEN: That's really humorous, Senator.

LEAHY: I'm talking about the volume, not the content. The nice thing about this ear protection, it lowers sounds to a normal level and it makes it more comfortable. Actually, the shooting makes it . . .

BIDEN: Sometimes, the older you get, the harder it is to hear. I'll speak louder. I didn't realize.

Eventually, finally, we voted down all the Biden amendments.

Not that we were out of the woods yet. There still remained several amendments, including one offered by Senators Graham and Kennedy that essentially would have gutted the entire bill. Behind the scenes, Senator Graham thought he had won the support of three fellow Republicans—Senators Grassley, Cornyn, and Kyl—and at least Kyl's vote was thought to be solid. At one point, I called an informal recess and proceeded to speak with all of these senators, urging them to at least vote the bill out of committee and reserve their objections for the floor. When the vote was called, every Republican senator voted no, including Kyl, following a noticeable pause. The result was such a surprise that Senator Graham asked after the vote, "Chairman, do people know they were voting on my amendment?" Finally, by midafternoon, when everyone was exhausted, the committee voted 13 to 5 to send a final bill to the floor for action by the full Senate. Several overworked staff members proceeded to exchange congratulations and hugs. I had not had lunch, but was satisfied that I was able to leave Capitol Hill by 2:40 in time for a train to Philadelphia, where I would attend an event honoring Shanin and Tracey at the Perelman Jewish Day School. All in all, the day got a C+/B– grade.

The effort to secure and submit asbestos legislation to the full Senate had entailed a frenetic pace of activity: Besides the numerous stakeholder meetings, hearings, and markups, I had to fit in whatever additional meetings I could with individual stakeholders and senators—in my main office, in my hideaway, wherever we could work toward a solution. Gary Slaiman, an attorney who represented a group of companies supporting the proposed national trust fund for compensating asbestos claimants at the stakeholder meetings, called the undertakings toward the bill "the most intensive legislative effort I have ever been involved with" in his nearly twenty-five years as a legislative practitioner.

Fighting with Joe Biden was especially difficult for me because he is perhaps my best friend in the Senate. For twenty-four years, we had ridden the train together from Washington. He would get off at Wilmington, and I would go on to Philadelphia. We had discussed all the problems of the world and found many areas of agreement. When the day was over, I think he realized the combined impact on me of Hodgkin's, chemotherapy, asbestos reform, and Joe Biden. He later telephoned with the longest apology I have gotten in my Senate career.

In essence, he said, Arlen, I feel terrible about what I've done. I know you were in pain, and I really apologize for the way I behaved.

"Forget about it, Joe," I replied. We were too good friends to let something like that fester or be taken too far. Besides, I had told some colleagues after my diagnosis that I would rather fight with them than fight the disease alone.

In a sense, the tougher the day, the better I liked it. It kept my mind off of me. It had nothing to do with my standing with my colleagues, because as Senator Leahy said of me,

> No senator, Republican or Democrat, would have criticized him, openly or behind closed doors, if he said, "Look, I'm just going away for two or three months till I feel better." Nobody would. He's paid his dues. He's been here a while. But instead, he made the decision that he would do a full day's work, and actually a full day's work for him is like two or three for some around here.

During my illness, I liked to quote Mae West: "When I'm good, I'm very good. But when I'm bad, I'm better." The illness was far from being a drain on my ability to work, and the Judiciary chairmanship opened the way for me to address issues that needed to be addressed. There were many of them. The issue of the treatment of al Qaeda suspects detained at the Guantánamo Bay prison facility was heating up, resulting in a four-hour committee hearing in mid-June. Since Mondays were slow in the Senate, with no floor action or hearings scheduled until late in the day to allow members to return from their home states, I scheduled a field hearing in Philadelphia on gang violence and a Philadelphia Bar Association speech on Mondays to be sure those days would be totally occupied. The reauthorization of the Patriot Act required a hearing in May and a markup session in July. Robert Mueller, the director of the FBI, was someone I regularly consulted during committee deliberations over the Patriot Act. Having witnessed his wife, a cancer survivor, undergo chemotherapy, he expressed astonishment that the cumulative effects of my own treatment did not diminish my involvement in Senate business. When I returned to HUP for additional tests on June 2, I received more good news: the PET scan remained negative, and the CT scan showed the nodes to be even smaller than the previous test.

On another front, *New York Times* reporter Judith Miller was jailed for eighty-five days on a contempt charge arising from her refusal to testify before a grand jury investigating the leak of the name of a possibly covert CIA agent. While the investigation ostensibly began as a national security matter, the immediate issue Miller allegedly might testify to was a perjury or obstruction of justice charge far removed from national security interests. In August, I visited her in the local detention center, where she appeared haggard—as I often did at the time!—and slept in a cell with a two-inch-thick mat for a mattress. Although she seemed tired and had bags under her eyes, she readily spoke with me about the need for a privilege for reporters and the objectionable nature of her detention—issues on which I shared many of her views. I had not known Miller before she became a national celebrity over this incident, but I had always respected the importance of investigative reporting in disclosing official corruption or incompetence. It certainly would have a chilling effect on investigative reporting to allow a reporter to be incarcerated for eighty-five days. I proceeded to hold two hearings on legislation to give reporters a qualified privilege not to reveal confidential sources, with reasonable exceptions such as actual national security threats. I thought then that the special investigator responsible for the jailing, Patrick Fitzgerald, had exceeded his authority. Subsequent revelations about the investigation suggest it was even more spurious than initially suspected, because it turned out that Fitzgerald had known that Richard Armitage, the deputy secretary of state, was the one who had disclosed the CIA agent's name, long before Miller was incarcerated.[21]

On reflection, I thought we ought to expand the Senate workweek. As matters stood, it was very difficult to convene a Monday morning hearing. Too often, the institution fell into a routine—irrespective of the party in control—of starting its workweek Tuesday at 2:15 after members finished their respective conference luncheons, and members started heading for the airports by midafternoon on Thursday. Why not increase the workweek to three days, which would be a 50 percent increase? I joked.

7

SEEKING CURES FOR OTHERS

WHILE MY JUDICIARY Committee chairmanship occupied most of the attention I received during my struggle with Hodgkin's, I still had a number of responsibilities relating to my chairmanship of the Appropriations Subcommittee on Labor, Health and Human Services, and Education. While I had this important platform to fight on public health issues for years, it added potency to the message that the messenger was ailing himself—something that had not occurred to me except as an afterthought. I often reflected on President Richard M. Nixon's declaration of war against cancer and thought that if we had devoted the same resources to that war that the United States does to other wars, we would have defeated cancer long ago. Perhaps my own Hodgkin's might have been prevented had we pursued cancer as relentlessly as we did Hitler and Saddam.

My passion for medical research did not begin with my Hodgkin's diagnosis. The subcommittee was one of my top choices after my first election to the Senate in 1980. In that capacity, I consistently supported increased funding for the National Institutes of Health (NIH), which rose from $3.6 billion in 1981 to $11.2 billion in 1994. After becoming chairman of the subcommittee in 1995, I took the lead with Senator Tom Harkin to increase NIH funding from $11.2 billion to $29.1 billion in 2006. I enjoyed a very productive relationship with him, as the subcommittee's ranking member. He is a kind and warm individual who shares my public health goals. During the 1990s, Tom helped me fight the Clinton administration to support increases in NIH funding, and in the 109th Congress, I helped him take on the Bush administration in getting the funding we sought to fight avian flu. He even voted against his party in favor of our asbestos bill. His reaction to my diagnosis was a large measure of sympathy, but he said I got by in my work because of what he called "Midwestern grit."

I have long opposed earmarking money for specific diseases, because the best judgment will be made by NIH scientists, not by members of Congress responding to pressures from groups who favor one ailment or another.[1] Watching the virtually miraculous results at the NIH in making major advances in fighting heart disease, cancer, stroke, and AIDS, I had become convinced the sky was the limit, and perhaps all maladies could be cured if we devoted sufficient resources to the goal. In 2005, only 1.1

percent of the federal budget of about $2.6 trillion went to the NIH, which was a little more than one-fifth of one percent (0.22 percent) of our gross national product. Our priorities were misdirected, considering that health is our nation's principal capital asset, indispensable to the "pursuit of happiness"—a national goal since the Declaration of Independence—and a major drain on the U.S. economy. It costs $1.7 trillion every year for treatment, so much of which could be saved through effective prevention. Most basic medical research in the United States is funded by the NIH, so the question of federal funding is critical. That is largely why I consider the NIH the crown jewel of the federal government. Close behind is the Centers for Disease Control and Prevention (CDC).

Because they have a platform and an audience, celebrities and other public figures are uniquely situated to send messages, whether implicit or explicit, to the public about illness and possible cures. The most prominent celebrity was Pope John Paul II, who died on April 2, 2005, after a long and visible struggle with Parkinson's disease. Besides being an advocate for world peace and an opponent of communism, the late pope sent an audience of billions an inspirational message about the enduring value of life while fighting the afflictions of disease. It was a message conveyed in large part through his decision to continue with his work despite his suffering. I consider it an honor to have been in his presence twice. His picture, shaking hands with Joan and me in the background, hangs in a prominent place in my Senate office.

Closer to home, well-known personalities such as Chief Justice Rehnquist and ABC News anchor Peter Jennings waged public fights against cancer. A certain camaraderie develops among cancer victims. Hockey great Mario Lemieux, the Canadian-born owner of the Pittsburgh Penguins, was diagnosed with Hodgkin's at age twenty-seven in 1992. He called in March to sympathize and tell me of his own experience in battling and beating Hodgkin's. It gave me a lift. Lemieux used his celebrity status to spread awareness of the need for cancer research.

When I heard Peter Jennings had lung cancer, I sent him a short note: "Very sorry to read about your problem. I've found the best response to the chemotherapy is to stay on the job. The hair loss and the rest of it is tough, but people understand." Peter referred to that note in a thank-you letter he wrote to well-wishers in late April: "Arlen Specter wrote me a note to say that the only way to get through chemo is to 'work your way through it.' He's a tougher man than I am." He illustrated his own difficulty: "Yesterday I decided to go to the office. I got as far as the bedroom door. Chemo strikes." Peter did not give himself credit, but his public struggle inspired many to learn of the dangers of smoking and to win their own fights with nicotine. Sadly, Peter died on August 7, 2005.

May 11 memorably brought a number of celebrities to the Senate on behalf of a variety of public health causes. Foremost among them was a 9:00 A.M. hearing on a bill that authorized $45 million for education and awareness of gynecological cancer that too often goes undetected by women until it is too late. The bill was dubbed Johanna's Law for a fifty-eight-year-old Michigan school teacher who died of ovarian cancer in 2000 after failing to detect the warning signs. The spokesperson for the bill that day was the actress Fran Drescher, who survived uterine cancer in 2000 and later wrote about the experience in her book, *Cancer Schmancer*. At the hearing, the ever feisty, nasal-sounding actress raised eyebrows with her testimony:

> This June 21st I will be five years well from uterine cancer, but for two years and eight doctors I was misdiagnosed and mistreated for a perimenopausal condition that I did not have. And even though uterine cancer is a very slow-growing and noninvasive cancer, it remains the only female cancer with a mortality rate that's on the rise.
>
> Women with ovarian cancer—who often are misdiagnosed and mistreated for irritable bowel syndrome—waste precious time because ovarian cancer is far more aggressive and fast-growing. 80 percent of all women with ovarian cancer will be diagnosed in the late stages, and 70 percent of them will die.
>
> How many women go for a second opinion when the doctor is telling them they are essentially fine? I did. I went for seven second opinions, as a matter of fact. I got in the stirrups more times than Roy Rogers . . .
>
> (LAUGHTER)
>
> . . . always telling the doctors my symptoms, but each time I slipped through the cracks. Initially I

experienced staining between periods and cramping after sex, but eventually my stool changed. I had tenderness under my arms and leg pains. One doctor told me to stop eating so much spinach. Another said I have the breasts of an 18-year-old, which I do.

"How is that relevant, Ms. Drescher?" I interjected. The audience laughed. The witness just continued:

And a third one told me to try gin and tonics before going to bed. So there I was, with perky breasts, in need of roughage, going to bed sloshed in some vain attempt to cure myself.[2]

Say what you will about that testimony, but everyone in the room left better informed about gynecological cancer. The actress and I were photographed shaking hands across the hearing room dais, and between my wrinkled, balding visage and her radiant appearance, we presented a stark contrast between being ill and being cured. In a follow-up e-mail, Drescher wrote me, "Your cancer, as with my own, I believe is proving to be an opportunity for true purpose. Remember there can be many silver linings in even the bleakest of clouds. Sometimes the best gifts come in the ugliest packages!" As to my work to secure more funding for cancer research, Drescher said: "This will be your finest hour."

Following the hearing on Johanna's Law, a Judiciary Committee markup on the asbestos bill regrettably kept me away from another subcommittee hearing on Lou Gehrig's disease, which featured the testimony of Tommy John and David Cone, two former members of the New York Yankees, Gehrig's team. Still later in the day, I met with Joan Rivers, a national spokesperson for osteoporosis prevention who was diagnosed with the brittle-bone disease in 2002. Ms. Rivers' message has gone beyond stopping the progress of the disease to actually educating people as to how to reverse its course. She did not allow her message to conceal her usual good humor. Ultimately, that day was eventful but tiring, meriting a grade of C for how I felt.

There is a unique quality about being on television that carries over from movies and the silver screen. Sunday morning TV shows and C-SPAN allow members of Congress to become minor celebrities. TV provides a platform to get public support for medical research. During my first hearing in 2005 to highlight the work of the NIH (on April 6), I used the event to personalize my own battle:

I have a lot of questions about my health. I had my fourth treatment last Friday and I am on the job. During the 2-week recess when I could not travel abroad, I was in Washington most of the time, and aside from an involuntary new hair style, I'm accommodating to all of the rigors of the situation. I find that among all of the alternatives, the best alternative is to come to work and fight tigers, and we've got a lot of tigers around here, and fighting tigers is a great distraction and a great cure. So just that little bit of recommendation to the foremost scientists in the world, just how to handle one person's temporary medical problem.[3]

I asked the first witness, Dr. Elias Zerhouni, "Is there any shortcut to . . . returning Arlen Specter the kind of head of hair that Elias Zerhouni has?" The NIH director, who had been there for me the day of my diagnosis, had a rich endowment of dark hair.

"I would be very happy to share," he replied.

"I don't want [to] share, I want my own," I added.[4] Privately, I would point out only half jokingly to some doctors that the stakes for them in keeping me alive were enormous. The medical profession, after all, relies so much on the NIH. Dr. Glick once told me in jest, "Senator, I've got to get you well, because you're the person at the barricades protecting the Republic."

"Will do, Dr. Glick," I replied. I frequently carried with me an hourglass given to me years earlier by Jim Cordy, a Pittsburgh constituent with Parkinson's disease. In 1999, Jim displayed an hourglass while testifying before the subcommittee as a reminder that those with Parkinson's were losing brain cells just as relentlessly as the sand slips from the upper chamber of the hourglass until empty. That would continue to happen as long as there was no cure. I used the hourglass as a prop for a photograph. It caught people's attention and dramatized Cordy's point that his life was slipping away and that medical research should intensify its efforts to find a cure and save his life.

My illness was obvious when a longstanding friend,

Jerry Zucker, paid me a visit in early April to get an update on the issue of embryonic stem-cell research. A Hollywood producer-director-writer with credits that included *Airplane!* and *Ghost,* Jerry had become active promoting stem-cell research in California, and he brought his seventeen-year-old daughter Katie, who suffered from diabetes. Jerry was shaken to see my frail appearance and watery eyes, which appeared sad to him. Upon expressing his concern, I told him and Katie, "I'm going to beat this," and that I would fight for more research. Movingly, Katie said that meeting a senator who suffered from Hodgkin's made her feel as if I understood her illness. I hope I did. Being a cancer patient gave me the best opportunity to seek cures for others.

The issue of embryonic stem-cell research would become a bone of contention in the 109th Congress. My voice, in much lower decibels several years ago, was the first one heard in the congressional debate on this subject. I scheduled the first subcommittee hearing on the subject in November 1998, ten days after stem cells first burst upon the scene. To keep up with fast-moving developments, the subcommittee has held twenty hearings on the subject through 2007. Stem cells are extracted from embryos used for in vitro fertilization. Generally, about a dozen are created in this procedure, only three or four are used, and the rest are frozen. As proponents of federal funding, Senator Harkin and I pointed to the limitless possibilities of using adaptable stem cells to replace diseased cells—holding out potential cures for a variety of degenerative diseases, including heart disease, Parkinson's, Alzheimer's, and, perhaps, all known maladies. In fact, when I mentioned the issue to my dentist, he told me that embryonic stem cells can help with root canal work. By injecting them into the canal having diseased tissue, the patient may be able to have a third set of teeth. While stem cells derived from adults and umbilical cord blood had produced advances of their own, scientists at the time widely considered them to lack the adaptability of embryonic cells.

More recently, the technology has shown promise in the exploration of possible cures for cancer, because stem cells have been found to be the source of at least some and perhaps all cancers. Several top scientists have found that tumors often regenerate after being nearly destroyed by cancer drugs, perhaps because the cancer cells possess the same properties as stem cells. If in fact the cells that are not destroyed by successful chemotherapy are cancer stem cells, different forms of treatment can be explored to target those cells. Since biologists are not yet certain how cancer cells are generated, more research is necessary, but this is an avenue that must be explored.[5]

Opponents of such research argue that destroying embryonic stem cells for use in research is the destruction of life. However, there are more than 400,000 frozen embryos, and those of us who support the research argue that we should use them to save lives instead of throwing them away. Agreeing that the best use of these embryos would be to create life if they were used for that purpose, I worked to appropriate $2 million to promote embryo adoption for fiscal year 2005. As of 2006, however, only approximately 200 out of 400,000 were utilized for adoption,[6] so the choice is to use or lose the vast majority that remained. Senator Harkin and I were joined by Senators Orrin Hatch, Dianne Feinstein, Ted Kennedy, and Gordon Smith in promoting legislation for federal funding for embryonic stem-cell research. Senator Hatch's joining was especially significant, because he was so well respected among the generally opposed pro-lifers.

Through the 1990s, there was a flat prohibition on federal funding for embryonic stem-cell research, but this began to change amid significant pressure in the spring of 2001, when sixty-one senators signed letters urging the president to lift the funding ban. I had oral commitments for votes from about twenty more senators who preferred not to put it in writing. Similar sentiment was evident in the House of Representatives. That may have prompted the president to promulgate an executive order in August 2001 allowing federal funding for only about sixty existing lines, saying it was permissible because the embryos had already been destroyed. Otherwise, President Bush strongly opposed our stem-cell efforts.

The lines the president approved for funding turned out to be insufficient, but after the 9/11 attacks, there was no oxygen left in Washington for anything but terrorism and Iraq. Stem cells, therefore, went to the back burner. The 2004 campaign gave me unique opportunities to speak with—really to lobby—President Bush during his frequent trips to Pennsylvania. It was the president's practice to invite members to his cabin in Air Force One for the forty-five-minute flight from Andrews Air Force Base to Pennsylvania and the approximately thirty-minute limousine ride to our destination, so it provided ample time to talk. His openness to all topics led to extensive discussions on NIH funding and embryonic stem-cell research, which he opposed on what he termed ethical grounds. One limo ride from the Pittsburgh airport to the downtown area produced an intense, if not heated, discussion on stem cells among the president, Senator Santorum, and me. Needless to say, the vote was two-to-one against.

On February 28, 2005, Senators Harkin, Hatch, Feinstein, Kennedy, and I reintroduced legislation to authorize federal funding for stem cell research. An identical House bill was introduced by Representatives Michael Castle, a Delaware Republican, and Diana DeGette, a Colorado Democrat. In May, as the House approached a floor vote on its bill, the issue increased in visibility just as I was changing from a robust, ruddy, healthy man with a full head of salt-and-pepper hair to a thin, pale, bald, sickly fellow. The Castle-DeGette bill passed on May 24, by a vote of 238 to 194, with fifty Republicans voting for it. The next day, Representative Castle came to the Senate Radio/TV Gallery with his bill authorizing federal funding for embryonic stem-cell research gift-wrapped with a red ribbon. In the widely circulated photos of the event, where I stood next to Senators Harkin, Kennedy, Feinstein, Hatch, and Smith in the background, I was totally bald.

The following Sunday, I appeared on *ABC This Week*, looking my worst after fourteen weeks of chemotherapy. The program, which originated from Tom Kline's beach house in Long Beach Island, New Jersey, gave me the opportunity to make a forceful case for federal funding of stem-cell research on national television. The other guest was Senator Brownback, an outspoken opponent of federal funding. I have long had a high regard for Sam's character, his thoughtfulness, and his sincerity across the board, but on this issue, I strongly disagreed. When I was questioned on the subject, I started by dissenting from President Bush's assertion that embryos are life, "because life does not occur until they're implanted in a woman." I then personalized the discussion by saying that if President Nixon's war on cancer "had been adequately funded like the rest of our wars, I might not have Hodgkin's lymphoma cancer today."

I broached the idea of "a march on Washington which would be the most massive in the history of the Washington Mall" to demonstrate to Congress the tremendous public support for embryonic stem-cell research. With some 110 million Americans affected directly or indirectly by diseases that possibly could be cured with embryonic stem cells, there has been the potential to mobilize sufficient public support to influence Congress to override any presidential veto. When it was his turn, Senator Brownback tried to make the point that life begins at conception.

He posed to me the following question: "When did your life start?"

I shot back, "Well Sam, I'm a lot more concerned about this point, about when my life is going to end."[7] That ten-second, emotional exchange evoked extensive public comment and has been replayed more than any sound bite I have been a party to in almost a half century of public life.

In subsequent interviews, I continued to personalize my stand on stem-cell research, even turning it up a notch. A June 3 news segment with Gloria Borger of CBS News introduced me as someone who "is no stranger to political controversy, but lately, he says he is a stranger to himself." Regarding the president's threat to veto the stem-cell research bill if it passed the Senate, Borger asked me, "Are you mad?"

"You bet," I replied. "I'm very angry that stem cells were not used in 1998, when we knew about them, but I'm really furious about the 110 million Americans who are suffering individually or their families who are suffering, and I think it is scandalous when we have the potential to save lives and we're not doing so."[8] An ABC News profile of me that ran on July 25 included the voiceover, "We were struck that the man at the center of [the stem-cell battle] is also fighting for his life." When the news station interviewed me, I went a step further than before in tying the government's foot-dragging to my condition: "They might well have found a prevention so that Arlen Specter didn't get Hodgkin's lymphoma cancer." The profile also included my basic advice to cancer patients: "Work, stay at work, it'll be the best thing you can do."[9]

On June 14, I had a chance to talk with the president alone for more than an hour on a flight from Andrews Air Force Base to Philadelphia and a drive to the suburbs for a Santorum fund-raiser. We focused on the House vote and a recent report on a possible breakthrough a few days later, a procedure that could harvest what were known as pluripotent cells, which might be able to behave like embryonic stem cells without entailing destruction of the embryo. The president was enthusiastic that this development might solve the ethical problem and allow federal funding. He added that he had tasked Karl Rove to talk to Nancy Reagan, widow of the former president and supporter of stem-cell research, and would follow through, depending on the results of further experimentation. In the interim, before that research could be completed, I urged the president to relax existing restrictions. The president remained unpersuaded, but said he was willing to discuss the matter further.

We had that chance later in the day as we flew, joined this time by Senator Santorum, to Penn State for a media event with the college's famed coach, Joe Paterno. I again urged the president to relax the stem-cell funding restrictions, but he took the stand that doing so entailed the destruction of life. I responded that I would never suggest using embryos for research if there were a chance to give them life, but these were going to be thrown away. I renewed my argument that there were 400,000 frozen embryos that would be discarded, only about 100 of which were adopted by then under the program we mutually supported. Thus, the choice did not entail taking life to preserve life, but rather to use or lose what would be discarded anyway. Rick interjected that the issue raised ethical, moral, and religious considerations that counseled against sanctioning the research with taxpayer funds. As before, I was outvoted, but I found my companions prepared to listen and open to extended discussion.

I remained interested in exploring as many avenues of research as possible, because scientists never know exactly which research will lead to the next great cure. I would later work with Rick on another bill to advance research of pluripotent stem-cell technology that did not entail embryo destruction. The year 2005 ended without a Senate vote on the Specter-Harkin bill because of the press of other Senate business and my being fully engaged in Judiciary Committee work, but the Senate would finally pass it in July 2006, by a vote of 64 to 36. Both houses lacked a veto-proof majority for the bill, and President Bush vetoed it as expected—the first veto of his presidency. The veto was sustained in the House by a vote of 235 to 193, fifty-one votes short of the two-thirds majority required to override. Although the Senate passed the alternative pluripotent stem-cell research bill, the House, apparently misunderstanding that the one bill was not a substitute for the other, rejected it.

When scientists in August 2006 announced a new method to conduct research on embryonic stem cells without injuring the embryo, my subcommittee got back to work with hearings to explore the new approach. The initial announcement turned out to be less than accurate, but I have long thought it is worse never to explore new possibilities than to do so and fall short. Persistence pays off, and surely enough, another development would be announced in November 2007: Two teams of scientists reported they had found a way to make human skin cells behave like embryonic stem cells without the need to make or destroy an embryo.[10] Whether or not this development alters the debate going forward, it could not change what happened a year earlier. Embryonic stem-cell research was an issue in the 2006 congressional elections and likely made the difference in the defeat of Senator Jim Talent of Missouri. The Santorum-Specter pluripotent stem-cell bill for its part was not enough to save my colleague. Rick would lose the election to Bob Casey, the son of the former governor. As it turned out, a single seat made the difference in control of the Senate.

8

PLAYING FOR THE AGES

S THE SUPREME Court term was about to end in June, rumors were swirling that Chief Justice Rehnquist would retire because of his cancer, and perhaps another justice would retire as well. Some speculated that Justice Sandra Day O'Connor was planning retirement to spend more time with her husband, John, who was in an advanced stage of Alzheimer's disease. When the Supreme Court issued its last decisions of the term on Monday, June 27, none of the justices announced their retirement. Then, in the early morning of that Friday, July 1, word came to me in my hideaway that Justice O'Connor had submitted a letter to the president stating her intention to retire upon the confirmation of her replacement. Her announcement was followed by a frenzy of activity by interest groups that sought to influence the process of nominating and confirming her replacement.

I had planned an early train back to Philadelphia, so I immediately scheduled a news conference for 11:00 A.M. to comment on the retirement. It had been the first time in eleven years that a justice retired, and given the mounting acrimony over lower court judges, the next Supreme Court nomination was expected to provoke a firestorm. I used the press conference as an opportunity to set a different tone: "The Judiciary Committee is prepared to proceed at any time, given a reasonable period of time for preparation. I've been through nine of these confirmation hearings; Senator Leahy has been through ten of them, so we know what to do." Yes, I acknowledged, replacing Justice O'Connor, who was a centrist swing vote in her judicial philosophy, "could produce more controversy" than the retirement of the chief justice, who was more firmly in the conservative bloc. However, I continued, "I don't want to prejudge anything. Our job is to sit back, conduct extensive hearings, give a thorough review to whomever is nominated, and to come forward with our committee report."

Questions continued about the effects of the recent confrontation over lower court nominees. Would we face "an even more involved and more confrontational situation involving a Supreme Court justice?" one reporter asked.

"Well," I responded, "I think the Senate learned a lot from the confrontation on the so-called constitutional or nuclear option and the right of filibuster. And as I have said before from this podium, I think the Senate made a wise decision in avoiding the controversy." This time around, "my own instinct is that we will not have a filibuster here. You really can't become involved in a filibuster on an eight-person court and have a four-to-four decision—so many are now five to four—you have a dysfunctional court. But let me repeat, that's only my hope."

What about the chief justice, whose illness was widely known? I responded with reference to his work on the Court: "Speaking as someone who likes to get up in the morning with something important to do, I wouldn't say that it's keeping the chief alive, but I think he likes his job. And if we haven't heard from him by now, the chances are you won't hear from him for some time." Then, inevitably, my own health came up:

Q: Mr. Chairman, you mentioned it's a very busy couple of months coming up. How are you feeling? How does this new obligation that's before you—does it invigorate you the way you assume that sometimes it invigorates the chief justice?

SEN. SPECTER: I feel—I feel fine. You haven't noticed any hesitancy in my responses?

Q: Not at all.

SEN. SPECTER: And except for my being the victim of identity theft, which I've talked to you about—I look in the mirror and can't believe that I saw myself on the front page of *USA Today* yesterday, and I said to my secretary, "Who is that unmasked man?"[1]

There were a few chuckles in the room. I continued, "But the energy level is high. Yesterday was 7 A.M. till midnight. This morning was a tough squash game, and I'm ready." In response to that quotation, my friend Arthur Makadon, a prominent Philadelphia lawyer and former assistant district attorney of mine, told the *Baltimore Sun,* "He's playing for the ages now, isn't he?"[2]

Following the news conference, I barely made my train to Philadelphia. I was looking forward to a week on Long Beach Island after a tense and tiring week, but instead would return to Washington Monday. The preparation for the Supreme Court nomination would allow no time off for the July 4 or August recesses. Senator Leahy and I agreed to work closely on a hearing schedule that would give adequate time for preparation and still be calculated to conclude the Senate's work in time to swear in the new justice by the end of September. That the road ahead would be rocky was clear from the day Justice O'Connor retired, when Senator Kennedy declared, "If the president abuses his power and nominates someone who threatens to roll back the rights and freedoms of the American people, then the American people will insist that we oppose that nominee and we intend to do so." Kennedy was moving right to the offensive. His tactic paralleled a notorious speech known as "Bob Bork's America" that he delivered within an hour after President Reagan nominated Judge Bork to the Supreme Court in 1987. When Senator Leahy and I appeared on *Meet the Press* two days later, I responded that

> it'd be very useful for the country if the rhetoric were to be toned down. I think when Senator Kennedy makes a statement that if the president doesn't make a nomination in accordance with Senator Kennedy's core views of the Constitution, that he's laying down a marker, you could say he's picking a fight. I don't think that's the best way to proceed. . . . If there is to be a fight, neither Pat Leahy nor Arlen Specter will run from it, but I think at the outset, the very day that Justice O'Connor retires to come up with fighting words isn't . . . the best way to approach the issue.[3]

"I agree with Arlen," Senator Leahy added. "Let's take it easy." I appeared on ABC's and CNN's Sunday news programs that same day to convey my point. It was going to be a busy season.

Our meeting at the White House to discuss the nomination process ended up taking place at 7:00 A.M. on July 12. Senators Frist, Reid, Leahy, and I were escorted into a small dining room adjacent to the Oval Office. Vice President Cheney and Chief of Staff Andy Card joined us at a table for seven. After some casual chitchat, the president thanked us for coming to talk about the Supreme

Court and called on me first. I remarked that I did not intend to put forward the names of any specific candidates, which would give me greater freedom and latitude, but I did suggest that he consider someone with a background that was diverse from those sitting on the Court. Justice O'Connor was the only sitting justice whose experience included serving as an elected official before becoming a judge, and she and the chief justice were the only two who were not elevated from a federal circuit court. On the issue of scheduling, I stated that the Judiciary Committee would be prepared to proceed in early August or September, and that it was our obligation to have the nominee in place by the start of the next session of the Court.

To the best of my knowledge, I was the only senator consulted by the White House on a list of fifteen prospective nominees. Harriet Miers, the White House counsel, called me at about 2:00 P.M. on July 18 and asked if I could come to the White House late in the afternoon to meet with her and Karl Rove on the "big subject"—which she did not have to identify by name. I responded that I could not get there until around 6:15 or 6:30 P.M., which she said would be fine. It was a stressful, complicated day, as usual, with a meeting at 5:00 P.M. convened by Senator Frist with committee chairmen followed by a 5:30 vote and 5:40 meeting in my hideaway with advocates of stem-cell research. The evening was further complicated by the fact that a long-delayed annual softball game between Senator Santorum's staff and mine was scheduled for 6:30 P.M. on the same evening—a "must appearance." First things first, however, and I was anxious to know what was happening on the selection of a replacement for Justice O'Connor.

After I arrived at the White House at about 6:30 P.M., Miers, Rove, and I sat down to go over the list of prospective nominees. We did so in alphabetical order, starting with Samuel Alito of the Third Circuit, and ending with J. Harvey Wilkinson of the Fourth Circuit. I offered my immediate views on those whom I knew and then called Miers the next day to comment on the others after making inquiries—in particular to Judge Becker, whose knowledge of the federal judiciary was encyclopedic.

Immediately after the White House meeting, however, it was time for softball. En route from the White House to the softball field a few blocks away, I changed in the car into khakis and a polo shirt. I pitched one scoreless inning, giving up only one hit and no runs due to outfielders with nimble gloves. In my one time at the plate, though I had not lifted a bat for some time, I grounded to third and was out at first base by twenty feet. ABC News, which was doing a profile on my response to cancer, recorded my pitching and hitting. I later saw on the video how gaunt I had become. My pitching looked okay, but my wobbly run toward first base on the grounder showed the toll Hodgkin's had taken.

It was clear the following day that President Bush had moved swiftly. His nomination announcement was imminent. NPR reported that he would nominate Judge Edith Clement of the Fifth Circuit at a 2:00 P.M. news conference, and Judge Clement's name circulated through Capitol Hill until some doubts were raised late in the afternoon. At about 5:00 P.M., I received a message inviting me to come with Joan to the White House between 8:30 and 8:45 P.M. to join the president in his announcement. Since Joan happened to be in town on her one-night-a-week visit to Washington, she was able to accompany me. I was told I would be the only member present.

At about 7:40, as I was on the Senate floor casting the last of three votes, a page called me into the cloakroom, a small anteroom off the main Senate floor where members can carry on discussions or use the telephone. Picking up the phone, I identified myself: "Arlen Specter here." The voice at the other end of the line jokingly said, "I thought this was Joan Specter." It was the president on the line, feeling pretty good and enjoying a little fun. He told me that he was going to announce D.C. Circuit Judge John Roberts for the Supreme Court vacancy. It had already made the news wires. Nothing stays secret in Washington. Without committing myself, I said I thought it was a good choice. The previous evening, I commented at the White House meeting that everything I knew about Roberts was positive. He had an excellent academic and professional background. Roberts had been nominated for circuit judge by President Bush the elder in 1992 and was pigeonholed by the Democrats despite his extraordinary ability as an appellate lawyer. That was a testament to the deterioration of the nomination process. His lack of an extensive paper trail prior to his appointment as a circuit judge by the younger Bush in 2003 aided his chances to join the Supreme Court.

I arrived at the White House just after 8:30 for the president's 9:00 public announcement of Roberts's nomination. As the only senator invited, which gave me some insight into how important the president and his advisers thought the committee chairman was in the confirmation process, I felt "buttered up." My hosts knew I would not be compromised by the red-carpet treatment. Joan, who is generally blasé about everything, was visibly excited, and kept telling me that evening and the next morning how much she enjoyed the event.

It was a unique experience, even after twenty-four years in Washington, to chat with the president, Laura Bush, Karl Rove, and Harriet Miers, together with Judge Roberts, his wife, and their two children in an exciting setting before a historic announcement. As usual, the best part of the event was missed by the TV cameras, which focused on the president and Judge Roberts to the exclusion of his beautiful six-year-old daughter and rambunctious four-year-old son, who was dancing and making faces while his father maintained his composure during the president's speech. His performance was reminiscent of my granddaughter Perri's dance on stage in Erie during my 2004 announcement tour. After the announcement, which occurred in the East Room of the White House, the group gathered for a brief conversation. President Bush was in an ebullient mood and was complimentary about my looks and energy level. He told Joan that he and I had spent quite a bit of "quality time" together. Judge Roberts and I talked about a lunch he and I had had years earlier with Allen Snyder, who had been nominated by President Clinton for the D.C. Circuit. Both men had had their nominations scuttled in the Senate, and I was very much impressed by both of them at that lunch as I asked them questions and they gave their views on the confirmation process.

The next day was largely occupied with Roberts hoopla, including a 9:00 A.M. news conference in the Senate Radio/TV Gallery, an afternoon presentation of the nominee to the news media along with Senators Frist and McConnell, and a private late-afternoon meeting with Roberts. I told reporters that I planned on holding fair, detailed hearings and that I hoped people would keep the rhetoric to a minimum and wait for Judge Roberts to be heard.

The reaction of interest groups to my role was interesting. A *Pittsburgh Post-Gazette* profile of me quoted Ralph Neas, president of the liberal organization People for the American Way, as stating that I held "perhaps the most important vote in the United States Senate." It then quoted Sean Rushton, president of the conservative Committee for Justice, as saying, "In a strange way he can be very effective because he does have a lot of credibility with moderates and liberals." The title of the article affirmed everyone's ambivalence about me: "Memories of Bork, Hill Make All Sides Uneasy."[4]

Attention to the Roberts nomination did not preempt the heavy Judiciary Committee schedule, which included a hearing on legislation to combat violence against women on Tuesday, a hearing on the reporter's privilege on Wednesday (which focused in part on Judith Miller's incarceration), and a markup session Thursday in which the Patriot Act reauthorization was reported out of committee. In fact, soon before Tuesday's nomination announcement, on a dual or triple track, Senator Frist scheduled a senators' meeting on stem cells to work out a schedule for floor action.

Two days after nominating Judge Roberts, President Bush convened a White House meeting to stimulate prompt if not immediate action on early hearings and an early Senate vote. Scheduling decisions are really the Senate's, with the chairman's prerogative to set the hearing date. I listened as President Bush, Vice President Cheney, Chief of Staff Andy Card, and Senators Frist and Mc-Connell advocated early Senate hearings to guarantee that Judge Roberts would be seated by October 3, the start of the Court's new term.

When the president and other participants advocated beginning the nomination hearings on Monday, August 29, I reminded them we first needed to determine the volume of Judge Roberts's paper trail to see how long it would take to prepare. I sensed there would be substantial and vocal objections from the Democrats, and equally intense but whispered reluctance from Republicans, to returning to Washington in advance of Labor

Day. As far as I was concerned, I said facetiously, my preferable starting date was August 1, because I needed something to occupy that day to cast off the effects of the chemotherapy.

It was important to start off without partisan bickering, I pointed out, because any senator could throw a monkey wrench into the proceeding at virtually any time. I voiced my own personal flexibility on either late August or early September for the start of the hearings, depending on the time required for preparation and a reasonable accommodation of committee members. Throughout that White House meeting, my mind was on the next day, when I would receive my last chemotherapy cocktail. I was still concerned that the cumulative effect of the twelve cocktails was going to catch up with me. There is a striking photo of the president and me shaking hands in advance of our discussion of the Roberts hearings. It shows me totally bald, thin, and pallid. The president is shaking my hand at a distance, sort of stretching, nearly turning away. I speculated he was thinking: *He's a good guy, but I don't think he's going to make it. What he has is not supposed to be contagious, but who really knows?*

From the White House, I returned to the Capitol to meet with Senator Leahy for more than an hour. He was adamant about starting the hearings September 12, arguing that people would want to stay home the day after Labor Day to take their children to school and that senators would need a week to clean off their desks. I found his arguments very unpersuasive, but I listened politely—a technique I have developed in my conversations with Pat and frankly with many others after becoming chairman. Before serving in that role, I had far more latitude not to suffer fools or even geniuses lightly, but the chairmanship carries an added responsibility if one wants to be effective and maintain smooth relationships. Our conversation was temporarily interrupted and resumed on the Senate floor during the evening's final vote, which had been scheduled around 6:45. We had limited time, because I had to leave for a dinner meeting in my condo with law professors, and Pat followed me into the corridor as I left the chamber.

As usual in the corridor, reporters swarmed around like bees on honey. They qualified as bees even though Pat and I hardly qualified as honey. We stood speaking for ten to fifteen minutes in the archway between the chamber and the corridor as the reporters lingered in the corridor. As soon as we moved to the elevator, they pounced on us, expressing concern that they could not lip-read and wanted to know what we were discussing. Scheduling, we replied. Although the issue was not resolved that day, September 6 was ultimately set as the start of the hearings, with an expectation that leadership would schedule subsequent floor action in time to reasonably assure a Senate vote before October 3. Although working out a detail like scheduling may seem relatively unimportant, Senator Leahy noted that senators considered it a display of a "level of civility and cooperation" between the parties that had not been "seen in the Senate in years."

The dinner meeting that night in my condo was the first of several I had arranged with noted law professors with the goal of giving myself a refresher course in constitutional law. Each of these meetings included a different pair of professors, typically of different philosophical leanings, who endured my overheated apartment to answer my questions and offer informed background. We touched on the parameters of questioning during the hearing and the doctrine of stare decisis that counsels respect for precedent. My greatest focus, however, was on a line of recent cases that questioned Congress's "method of reasoning" in passing a number of laws we deemed important to redress serious problems—particularly the Religious Freedom Restoration Act and the Violence Against Women Act.

I was outraged when I read these opinions by unelected judges who were summarily dismissing the product of extensive fact-finding that had been conducted by those of us whom the people elected. In fact, our current efforts with respect to the violence against women legislation were an attempt to satisfy a Supreme Court decision in 2000 that held the previous act unconstitutional. In two cases decided by a five-to-four margin, the Court even took a jurisprudential swing at the Americans with Disabilities Act, holding in 2001 that it was unconstitutional in an employment discrimination case when applied to a woman who had breast cancer and then holding in 2004 that it was constitutional in an access case when applied to a paraplegic who had to crawl up the steps to access a courtroom.[5]

My final chemotherapy treatment on July 22 was sandwiched between my first law professors meeting the night before and the second on Monday the twenty-fifth. Professor William Eskridge of Yale Law School said I was "like a prosecutor" and inquisitive during the first meeting, but during the second, Professor Mark Tushnet of the Georgetown Law Center found me listening more than questioning. That was consistent with the cyclical fatigue caused by chemo. I kept playing squash, though I suffered a bad fall on the court on Tuesday, July 26. Although I do not think I was worse following the final treatment than after previous ones, Shanin and Tracey found me paler and more fatigued than ever.

The following Sunday, I began an exhausting day on the squash court with Evan Kelly before he drove me to a television studio in Philadelphia, where I would appear on *Face the Nation* to discuss stem cells and the Roberts nomination with Senator Brownback. As we approached the studio, I spotted a space where we could parallel-park the car. "Park here," I told Evan. He was struck by how little space there was, but figured he would try it since I was the boss. I was confident in my judgment of distance since my teenage days driving a truck in the Kansas oil fields. My father's junkyard had narrow paths riddled with sharp, potentially tire-cutting objects, and my experience gave me a feel for judging parking spots that stayed with me. It took my incredulous driver five minutes of pivoting and weaving to make it into the spot, at which point there would be only a few inches to spare on either side of the car. I didn't think anything of that minor incident, but it made quite an impression on him because he quoted me repeatedly to office associates: "There's a lesson for you to learn here. Keep going, and you can do it."

The next day, I went back to HUP to have another CT scan and PET scan—the first to follow the completion of my treatments. For the first time, the tests showed, as I triumphantly wrote in my datebook calendar, "*no trace* of Hodgkin's." Dr. Glick declared me in "complete remission." That had been his informal opinion following the tests on April 8, but now it was official. There is always a certain amount of tension awaiting test results. It is an all-day process without any sleep, and by the end of the day the anxiety level is so high that it is quite a relief to hear a positive pronouncement from the doctor.

While I could not clinically be considered cured until five years elapsed from the end of therapy without recurrence of the disease, this was as good as things could get for now. Dr. Glick then commented on how remarkable he thought my tolerance was to the treatment, saying I was "in the top 5 percent of people who have ever had this chemotherapy" at my age.

"Is that all?" I responded semifacetiously.

Dr. Glick quickly revised his statement: "Never in my thirty-four years in practice have I ever seen someone your age tolerate aggressive chemotherapy treatment that well with fewer side effects than people half your age." That was more like it. Senator Coburn, my "second doctor" and a tough cancer survivor in his own right, was very supportive and complimentary about my response to chemotherapy. He bucked up my spirits by repeatedly making comments to the effect that I was "the toughest guy he ever saw—tough physically, tough intellectually, and tough emotionally."

Notwithstanding the favorable tests, I was fatigued during the first week of August, which I spent at my desk at home in Philadelphia preparing for the Roberts hearing. On Saturday, I skipped dinner and wrote in my datebook, "totally exhausted—never so tired." That was only the second day I gave myself an F.

When Roberts's opponents could not find anything adverse in his record, the organization NARAL Pro-Choice America became desperate and ran a TV advertisement accusing him of "supporting . . . a convicted [abortion] clinic bomber" and of embracing an ideology that "leads him to excuse violence against other Americans"—all based on his participation in a civil case while in the Justice Department that did not even involve clinic bombing. On August 12, I wrote the organization, which I had long supported, calling the ad "blatantly untrue and unfair" and asking that it be withdrawn. *The New York Times* noted that even "[s]ome prominent Democrats said they agreed with Mr. Specter. Lanny Davis, a top official in the Clinton administration, . . . called [the advertisement] 'inaccurate, filled with innuendo and shameless.'" The ad was quickly withdrawn.

By mid-August, Dr. Glick gave me permission to travel, which provided me a welcome break from Roberts and a chance to attend to some other Senate duties. I began with a trip with Joan to Cuba, which presents lingering dilemmas of effective drug interdiction and human rights abuses. While there I toured the U.S. prison facility at Guantánamo Bay, after long anticipating the opportunity to see for myself the place that had generated so much concern. My visit convinced me that congressional oversight and legislation were needed. Although Senator Durbin and I introduced legislation a few weeks after the September 11 terrorist attacks, Congress largely punted the issues surrounding the fate of detainees to the courts. They were simply too hot to handle at the time. I had long thought Guantánamo required congressional oversight, and I had held the June hearings after carefully reading three Supreme Court decisions from 2004 on the detainee issue.

I traveled to Guantánamo with the intention of conducting a field hearing to find out directly from interrogators and detainees what was going on. I arrived thinking I had a commitment from the Department of Defense, which administers the facility, to hold the hearing, but I learned upon arriving that it would not happen. Department staff in Washington claimed they had informed their Guantánamo staff, but those staffers explained, terrified, that they were never told about any hearing plans. I felt the rug had been pulled out from under me, but I made the best of my visit. I visited a building used for interrogation and met with a group of interrogators who were assigned to work with Saudi prisoners. I asked them about the tactics they used, and they were adamant that they did not use coercive tactics. They added that such tactics do not work. On the contrary, they said they found it most effective to develop a relationship with a detainee, treating him with respect and winning him over through positive reinforcement.

After Guantánamo, I visited courageous Cuban dissidents in Havana before my third meeting with Fidel Castro. I have long believed that dialogue with all foreign leaders, even our toughest adversaries, is important. In previous trips, I had pressed Castro on some of the most controversial issues involving our two countries: the Cuban Missile Crisis, the Kennedy assassination, and the assassination attempts against him. When I broached the theory postulated by some that he had been involved in the Kennedy assassination in retaliation for the president's authorization of the Bay of Pigs invasion, Castro denied any involvement and replied, "I'm a Marxist, not a crazy man."[7] Having just come from a meeting with dissidents, I pressed Castro to release the political prisoners in his jails. I also pressed him to open his country to democracy and dissent. He listened, but my exhortations had no effect.

From Cuba, I flew to Venezuela, where I met with prodemocracy critics of President Hugo Chávez who were being prosecuted by the government as an act of political intimidation. I then visited Chávez himself and discussed the importance of Venezuelan oil to the United States and the world, as well as our shared interest in drug interdiction. In the wake of a controversy over drug enforcement in which the Venezuelans refused to meet with the U.S. ambassador, I told Chávez that the parties to the controversy should be able to put the facts on the table and work toward a new protocol on drug enforcement. Fortunately, he agreed. Leaving Caracas, I felt more members of Congress should travel there and more U.S. diplomatic efforts should be undertaken to find ways our two countries could cooperate on issues of mutual concern.

I subsequently took the drug issue to officials in Costa Rica, where I met with drug enforcement officials. I later visited Dr. Rolando Herrero, a cancer researcher who was a pioneer in the exploration of the connection between viral infections and cancer. Dr. Herrero proved the connection between the human papiloma virus (HPV), a sexually transmitted disease, and cervical cancer, and was developing (with $5 million support from the National Cancer Institute) an HPV vaccine that could go a long way toward the protection of women's health.

Our final stop was Mexico City, where I met with then-president Vicente Fox, the Mexican attorney general, and other government officials to discuss immigration. Fox is an impressive man who did an outstanding job for his country. We agreed the war on drugs could not be won until we reduced "demand," but concurred that we should continue the fight against "supply." His insights proved helpful when the Judiciary Committee wrote a bill on immigration reform. Although tiring, I was able to maintain a high energy level in the nine-day trip and found it a refreshing diversion from Washington and the Roberts nomination.

Two days after returning from my trip, I was interviewed by Gwen Ifill of the *NewsHour with Jim Lehrer* for a profile for public television in advance of the nomination hearings. By that time, a trace amount of fuzz was returning to my head, and the interview started and ended with my cancer and chemotherapy:

> I have completed the chemotherapy. And during the course of the chemotherapy from February through July, I've been able to keep all my duties. I haven't missed a beat. As I've said in the past, I've beat a lot of tough opponents. I beat a brain tumor. I beat bypass surgery. I beat a lot of tough political opponents. And I'm beating Hodgkin's cancer as well. I'm fine.[8]

This was basically the same statement I made the week of my diagnosis, except now the last part was phrased not as a prediction, but in the present tense. In fact, by that time, I no longer assigned grades for how I felt each day.

The following week brought the first of two unexpected events which would change the scheduling for the Roberts hearings. On August 29, Hurricane Katrina hit the Gulf Coast hard and deluged much of New Orleans. The city's mayor, Ray Nagin, and Senators Leahy and Kennedy called me to urge the postponement of the Roberts hearing so the Senate could take up emergency relief legislation for the hurricane victims. I told Senator Leahy that I did not think the delay was warranted. If there was something that our committee members could do to help in the cleanup, or if there was some reason the hearings were impeding that effort, then I would certainly consider a delay. However, it seemed to me we ought to proceed in regular order and do our business as the American people and those in the devastated area would expect.

Then, at 11:55 P.M. on Saturday, September 3, three days before the Roberts hearings were scheduled to start, my communications director, Bill Reynolds, awakened me from a deep sleep in Long Beach Island to inform me that the chief justice had died. This introduced a new reason for a postponement. I thought of the Yiddish saying of my maternal grandmother, Freda Shanin: "*Mensch tracht und Gott lacht,*" Man plans and God laughs. Within eighteen hours of Rehnquist's death, I had three telephone conversations with Andy Card on scheduling and a new subject that opened up the most significant development of all. In the first telephone conversation with him that Sunday morning, I prefaced my comments by saying that I did not want to be presumptuous, but it occurred to me that the president might have been considering Roberts for the chief's position when the initial speculation was on Rehnquist's retirement, not O'Connor's.

With the chief's position now open, I pointed out that Roberts might be just the right person to build a consensus on the Court and move away from so many five-to-four divisive decisions. I noted that Roberts had shown a remarkable sense of self-confidence in describing his appearances before the Court as a "dialogue among equals." From the favorable responses Roberts had received from senators, including Democrats, I told Card that I thought his nomination for chief justice would be well received. Card then asked a strange question: "Do you mind if I share your idea with the president?" "Of course not," I responded, since it seemed obvious that I had made the suggestion for the president's consideration.

Card called back twice asking more questions focusing on the Democrats' potential reaction to the nomination of Roberts for chief justice. I reiterated I thought the reaction would be favorable. The final call at about 6:00 P.M. came at Tom Kline's home where I was playing squash. That night, exhausted from the hectic events of the day, the telephone's constant ringing, and the lingering effects of the chemotherapy, I unplugged the telephone in my Long Beach Island home. The next morning, at about 7:20 A.M., Tom Kline awakened me with a knock at the door. When I let him in, he said that Andy Card was trying to reach me and had called Tom's number, when Card found my phone continually busy. I called Card back immediately at about 7:25. He told me to turn on the television set, because the president was making an 8:00 A.M. announcement of Judge Roberts's nomination for chief justice. In the midst of heavy criticism of the administration's mishandling of Hurricane Katrina, the Roberts nomination for chief justice was a showstopper that dominated Labor Day television and the headlines for several days.

I called Senator McConnell after speaking with Andy Card, since the chief of staff had told me McConnell was totally opposed to any delays. I also thought it important to get McConnell's views and to let him know he was being appropriately consulted. When we spoke, McConnell was adamant that we not delay the hearings. He said I should use my scheduling power to "grind the Democrats down." I told him that it was a different ball game with Roberts now being nominated for chief justice. Technically, the president would have to send the Senate a new nomination, because it was a different position. I told McConnell that I would negotiate to try to start the hearings on Thursday since Rehnquist's funeral was set for 2:00 P.M. on Wednesday. When I spoke with Senator Leahy, however, he insisted on observing a Judiciary Committee rule requiring one week's notice for a hearing.

The events raised a new question whether it would be possible to have Roberts seated by the start of the new term on October 3. After checking with committee Democrats, Leahy informed me they were unwilling to make commitments, but would act in good faith to try to get the Senate votes done in time to seat Roberts, if confirmed, by the start of the new term.

The Roberts hearing began September 12, some seven and a half weeks after my final chemotherapy treatment. I felt considerably better and looked better. When you are as bald, pale, and gaunt as I was, you have no place to go except up, but the improvement in my appearance was too slight to convey to observers that they were looking at a healthy man. My voice continued to be raspy. It had not regained its old resonance. A few strands of hair were now barely noticeable. My eyes continued to water, but less than before, and I drank less Gatorade in public.

Still, the issue of my health was on center stage. The morning of the first day of the hearing, correspondent Ed Henry of CNN's *American Morning,* opened his comments with how Roberts would respond on abortion rights and quickly moved to my health: "Another interesting story line here will be how Senator Specter holds up. While he's chairing these hearings, he will be battling cancer." I admitted my problems:

It's tough. And every day, candidly, it's difficult to get out of bed.

HENRY: Arlen Specter can barely recognize himself in the mirror. Hodgkin's Disease has taken his hair.

SPECTER: And I've lost eight, 10 pounds because it's hard to eat in the few days following the chemotherapy treatments. There's a need for a lot of sleep.

HENRY: Specter has had little time to rest, prepping for the grueling task of chairing the confirmation hearings for John Roberts. But he says hard work is the best therapy.

SPECTER: When I'm not fully engaged, then this headache comes over me, my eyes tear. I've made Kleenex wealthy, I've made Gatorade wealthy, trying to keep from being dehydrated.

HENRY: Specter, who was diagnosed in February, recently finished the chemo and says he's feeling better.[9]

I needed all the energy I could muster for the four long days presiding over the Roberts hearings. Even during the toughest days between February and August, I had been able to summon enough energy to stay on top of my duties, but this hearing was tougher. There were no breaks when I could slip away for a nap. As chairman, I had to remain constantly on my toes in order to keep the hearings and my colleagues under control. Still, remarkably, the work was good for me. There is nothing the chairman can do during hearings but sit and preside. But presiding demands attention. When a member offers to have a document submitted for the record, as routinely occurs, the chairman must be alert to say "without objection," which then makes the document a part of the record. I missed just one such call during the hearings, only to read about it in the newspapers.

It is a delicate balance—a tough judgment call—to decide the leeway permitted to a senator when interrogating a nominee. Senators with long-winded speeches and meandering questions were not known to excel in hearings,[10] but such tendencies were unfortunately common enough to make it difficult to draw the line at times. Other than opening statements, the hearings are ostensibly designed to elicit answers from the nominee, but too often the senators who profess eagerness to hear from a nominee end up giving him or her little time to speak during the hearing.

To reflect the importance and bipartisan nature of the hearing, I departed from committee practice, which permits the majority party to call most of the witnesses, and allocated an equal number of slots to both parties. This comported with my father's advice about accommodation: When in a partnership, give 60 percent, because it will look like 50 percent to the other guy. If you give 50 percent, it will look like 40 percent. Always give more.[11]

Senator Kennedy spent a bit of his time during the hearing speechifying but had tough, well-prepared questions for Roberts. In an institution filled with oratory and some showmanship, Kennedy has a sincere, sometimes bombastic passion when he speaks in the Senate chamber. He pressed Roberts very hard on civil rights—so much so that he would not let him answer. Thinking about it in advance, I decided not to intervene to protect the nominee unless the senator went clearly over the line. On a couple of occasions, Kennedy came close, but I did not have to intervene to get Kennedy to let Roberts respond. Body language can be influential in a Senate hearing as well as other places. When Kennedy came close to the line, I would lean forward with my gavel raised, and Kennedy would ease off. During Senator Biden's opening round of questions, during which he spoke for more than twenty of his thirty allotted minutes, he inquired about Roberts's thinking on Title IX, which bans sex discrimination in educational programs. When Biden cut Roberts off, I intervened:

CHAIRMAN SPECTER: Now, wait a minute. Let him finish his answer, Senator Biden.

SENATOR BIDEN: The answers are misleading, with all due respect.

CHAIRMAN SPECTER: Well, they—

SENATOR BIDEN: Let me get—

CHAIRMAN SPECTER: Wait a minute, wait a minute. They may be misleading, but they are his answers. [12]

Roberts's opponents later put out a statement to the effect that I said Roberts was misleading the committee. I replied it was Roberts's opponents who were guilty of misleading since I had carefully said "may," not "were." I made it a point to tell Roberts during the next day's hearing that my statement "was in the subjunctive, and I was not suggesting that" his answers "were misleading." [13]

Surprising praise came from two committee Democrats who were well known for partisan warfare. Senator Schumer remarked, "I want to commend you and Senator Leahy. You are being fair and we are getting a full opportunity to ask questions." Senator Durbin added, "[T]hank you for your fairness."[14]

Those four days of nationally televised hearings produced a great deal of commentary about my appearance and vitality. Some people who had seen me on the Sunday talk shows weeks earlier noted the emerging hair, healthier complexion, and more robust voice projection. Many identified themselves as having cancer, and I was moved to hear people say they were inspired by my decision to stay on the job during the illness. "If you can do it, so can I" was the message I would hear, and not only from cancer patients. So many healthy members of the Senate family and my own staff would tell me they did not feel like coming to work some days, but if I could do it, so could they.

Curiously, my hair was the focal point of conversation. As soon as it started to return, my nine-year-old granddaughter, Perri, who had asked months earlier about my 70 percent chance of recovery, said: "Does your hair coming back mean you are cured?" Senator Pat Roberts, who is completely bald himself, repeatedly insisted I keep my hair short, because it made me look ten years younger. Others said twenty years younger; President Bush said twelve years younger. Senator Hillary Clinton told me that her mother wanted me to keep my hair short.

The boomerang of the NARAL ad and the absence of a smoking gun in the Roberts papers left the Democrats without much traction going into the hearings, and the nominee was so impressive throughout the hearings that there was no ground for the opposition to gain. Not only did he come off as knowledgeable and eloquent, but in my view, he answered more questions than many of his predecessors. Even Senator Biden called him "one of the best witnesses that . . . has come before this committee."[15] Some observers noted his almost Hollywoodesque presence, and beyond his appearance and poise, he possessed the substantive talent and professional background that made him a good fit to be chief justice. While many expected pretty much a party-line vote on the Roberts confirmation—indeed, Roberts himself told me the following year that was his expectation—a number of Democrats defied the conventional wisdom by expressing their support after the hearings concluded. The confirmation of a Supreme Court justice may well be the gravest responsibility to face the Senate short of deciding whether to go to war, and Senator Leahy displayed his own statesmanship by deciding to vote to confirm Roberts. As he later remarked, he and I "were both well aware of the fact that this was for chief justice of the United States, and the country's not helped by it looking like it's totally a party-line vote." The two Wisconsin senators—Herbert Kohl and Russ Feingold—voted for Roberts. So the committee vote was thirteen to five to report the Roberts nomination favorably to the full Senate.

A filibuster never became an issue, and exactly half of the Democrats voted to confirm. With all one hundred senators taking their seats to cast their vote for the first time in years, the vote tally was 78 to 22 with Senator Jeffords, nominally an Independent, voting aye. The moment made for a rare, certainly unexpected show of significant bipartisanship in a polarized age. Within my own party, things were more harmonious than one would have expected less than a year earlier. "Specter Rises Above 2004 'Worst Republican' Title," proclaimed a *Washington Times* headline. Former attorney general Ed Meese, who had endorsed Toomey in 2004, called me a "strong chairman" who he expected to handle the hearings "very fairly" even before they were completed. "In the context of this confirmation hearing, he has been spectacular," remarked Leonard Leo, executive vice president of the Federalist Society, the preeminent professional organization of conservative lawyers.[16] "I have gained new respect for the guy under his current circumstances," Sean Rushton of the Committee for Justice proclaimed. Even Reverend Patrick J. Mahoney, who had shouted, "Senator Specter must not assume that position!" on national news in November, now had this to say: "There were real concerns about Senator Specter's judicial agenda. . . . Looking back, I would have to say Senator Specter has done a fairly good job."[17] Despite the hearing delay caused by Rehnquist's death, the new chief justice, age fifty, took his seat on the first day of the new Supreme Court term, as had been the goal.

To convey the lasting impact of the action the Senate had just taken, Michael O'Neill, my chief counsel, asked our staff for a show of hands: Who here is thirty or older? Several hands went up, and O'Neill continued, "Sorry. None of you will ever be chief justice."

9

THE MISSION CONTINUES

BECAUSE ROBERTS FILLED only one of two Supreme Court vacancies, the pressure would remain on the Judiciary Committee as long as it took to fill the second vacancy, which turned out to be longer than many expected. Even before the Roberts nomination was a closed deal, President Bush was eager to move ahead with someone to replace Justice O'Connor, whose retirement was conditioned upon her successor being confirmed. The president scheduled a 7:00 A.M. meeting for Wednesday, September 21, to discuss the next nominee, even though we had not voted Roberts out of committee and floor action had not been scheduled. Anticipating the president's insistence on proceeding immediately, I called Andy Card shortly before noon on Monday the nineteenth to tell him that I thought the next hearing, if it came immediately, would be a bloodbath, and it would make a lot more sense to have Justice O'Connor stay on until June. I had drafted a letter to the justice setting forth my reasons for requesting her to stay on.

Card was immediately negative on the idea, advancing the argument that a new justice could decide cases even if he or she had not heard the arguments. I told him he was wrong about that. He then asked me if I was asking him if I should send the letter or informing him, and I replied that I was informing him. To keep the pressure on, President Bush called me shortly after I hung up with Card and expressed his appreciation for doing a good job on the hearings. I then told him my thoughts about O'Connor, though I am sure he already was informed, and he said that he would relish a good fight. I reminded him that I never ran from a fight, but I was concerned about getting his nominee confirmed. He suggested that O'Connor might not be anxious to continue to serve, and I replied that it was worth a try. He concluded the conversation saying, "Well, do what you got to do," with the negative implication ringing in my ears as our conversation ended.

I then called Justice O'Connor the following day, September 20. The justice told me she would be willing to serve until June if she were asked to do so, presumably by the president, and that she entirely agreed with me that the next confirmation hearing would be difficult. I used the term "bloodbath," and she agreed. While it was true that there would remain barely sufficient votes on the Court to reaffirm *Roe v. Wade* even if Roberts and the next nominee joined Justices Scalia and Thomas in voting to overrule it, that possible scenario was perilously close enough to fill the Senate cloakroom with rumors about heavy-handed opposition tactics on the next nominee.

When President Bush, Vice President Cheney, Andy Card, and Senators Frist, Reid, and Leahy and I had our September 21 meeting, I stated my case for deferring the nomination to the following year and noted that Justice O'Connor was amenable to staying on. The only response to my comments came from Senator Frist, who said he thought we ought to go ahead on schedule with the next nomination. We then went into suggestions regarding the next nominee. Senator Leahy advocated looking beyond the "judicial monastery," and Senator Reid agreed, suggesting Harriet Miers. Reid did not comment on her qualifications, noting only that she was a nice person and returned telephone calls promptly—hardly the strongest substantive recommendation.

In response to questions, I then offered comments on some of the candidates on the president's short list, explaining why I thought they would run into problems in the confirmation hearing. The president pressed as to my sources and I candidly responded. I stated that I had spoken with Carolyn Dineen King, chief judge of the Fifth Circuit, the jurisdiction from which three of the top female prospects for the court sat. The president asked me if she called me or I called her. I responded that Judge King had initiated the matter by contacting a mutual friend, Judge Becker, who contacted me, suggesting Judge King would be responsive to my call. As before, I did not initiate any suggestions as to who the nominee should be. Senator Schumer and Senator Reid notified the president separately of prospective nominees who would be filibustered.

On the morning of October 3, the president nominated Harriet Miers to fill the vacancy. The announcement was made in the solitude of the Oval Office at 8:00 A.M., within hours of the first session of the Roberts Court, and lacked the ceremonial atmosphere of the Roberts announcement in the East Room in July. In a press conference that day in the Senate Radio/TV Gallery, I was cautiously optimistic about the new nominee: "[E]verything I know about Ms. Miers is good, but I do not know a great deal about her professional activities or her academic standing or her work in her legal career, which appears to be a very distinguished career." Indeed, although she had not served previously as a judge—which can be said for thirty-eight past Supreme Court justices when they took their seats—she had been the head of the Dallas and Texas Bar Associations. Her résumé lent itself to comparison with former justice Lewis Powell, another nonjudge and a former American Bar Association president at the time he was nominated by President Nixon in 1971. In the present environment, however, her relative lack of a paper trail would raise doubt about her qualifications and ambivalence in all camps as to her judicial philosophy.

I told David Kirkpatrick of *The New York Times* that Miers could use a "crash course in constitutional law,"[1] but also emphasized the importance of letting the hearing process play out in committee. Instead, as I asserted on

ABC This Week on October 9, we faced "not a rush to judgment" with respect to Miers, but "a stampede to judgment." By that time, my illness was receding into yesterday's news, but I had a resurgence of the fatigue and eye watering I had felt throughout my treatment during the week following that October 9 interview. The chemotherapy overhang remained with me the next Sunday, the sixteenth, when I attended the unveiling of Paula Kline's tombstone. I still appeared ill to her husband Tom that day, and he wondered whether I was pondering my own mortality, given that the cemetery plot reserved for Joan and me rested beside Paula's. On this occasion, however, I thought nothing of my own future, but spent that somber occasion returning to her burial and thinking in anger about the tragedy of a death that is preventable. At that moment, it seemed to me like manslaughter at the hands of a society that had recklessly disregarded the steps it could have taken to conquer cancer.

That day soured my mood, and the next two weeks did little to sweeten it. Skepticism surrounding the Miers nomination seemed to snowball in Washington with every passing day, and the media conveyed the punditocracy's negativity from every ideological direction. I felt a great deal of personal tension amid the stampede to judgment on Miers. It did not help that her answers to the customary questionnaire sent by the Judiciary Committee to all nominees were deficient and had to be returned. On Thursday, October 27, a week and a half before her hearings were scheduled to begin, she asked the president to withdraw her nomination, no doubt under the mounting pressure within the Beltway.

I went to the Senate floor to decry that fact that "our constitutional process was not complete" and that "a one-sided debate in news releases, press conferences, radio and TV talk shows, and the editorial pages" denied her an opportunity to demonstrate her qualifications. Whether or not I or other committee members ultimately would have voted for her confirmation, she deserved that chance. I noted the event in my datebook with a single word—"disgrace." President Bush was not pleased. "Washington could be such a harsh and ugly town," he later told a member of my staff, but he appreciated that I had "respected Harriet's dignity." He called me in the Senate cloakroom the evening the withdrawal was announced and was profuse in his thanks for the treatment my staff and I had given Miers. He explained that he loved her, did not ask her to withdraw, and would not do anything contrary to her interests. I told the president that I was personally very offended by the treatment given the nominee, that she had been tarred and feathered and run out of town on a rail. That was only figuratively true, because she actually stayed on as White House counsel and selflessly served as liaison with the committee for her replacement—a true class act.

The nominee who replaced Miers was Judge Samuel Alito, a fifteen-year veteran of the Third Circuit. He was swiftly announced along with a request from President Bush that the Senate confirm him by end of the year. We had been on track to confirm Miers by Thanksgiving, but the president's scheduling request for Alito was unrealistic. It simply did not allow sufficient time to review the judge's approximately 3,750 cases, 300 opinions, and the balance of his voluminous paper trail in two months. I tried to explain this to Andy Card in a November 3 telephone conversation, and he replied I would have to tell the president myself—which, of course, I was glad to do.

Card then put me through to the president, who was in Argentine airspace en route to Buenos Aires, so the connection was not terribly good. I then repeated to the president the realities of reviewing Judge Alito's record. I added that he had the advantage of never having been a senator, so he had not seen firsthand how a single senator could throw a monkey wrench into the proceedings. I spoke of the chilly reception I had gotten from my Judiciary Committee colleagues on both sides of the aisle on the scheduling issue. I reminded him that the committee in general, not including myself, was exhausted after having worked since July on the Roberts hearing, virtually losing the August recess, followed by the intense hearings and further proceedings. We had then prepared for the Miers hearing to the point that we were all set to go, with opening statements and questions ready. It may have been the bad telephone connection or perhaps the intensity of our conversation that raised the decibel level of our conversation, but in the end, the president could only acquiesce. I was not sure about the tone of our telephone conversation until Card called me the next day to say the president and I did not have a shouting match. I replied that if that was his story, I'd stick to it. A *Washington Post* headline that appeared that day read, "Specter Bucks White House on Alito."[2] For my part, I would have liked to start the hearings on January 2, 2006, and take the committee vote by the thirteenth to ensure Alito's most reasonably prompt arrival on the Court in the event of confirmation. Since it was the right of every senator to hold over the committee vote for a week, I decided to start the hearings on January 9 with a good-faith understanding from the Democrats that the committee vote would occur on the seventeenth.

I had known Judge Alito casually during his tenure on the Third Circuit. Judge Becker had invited our wives and us to a dinner one evening. During my July 18 meeting in the White House regarding the president's short list for the Court, I remarked that I thought Alito was able and a good prospect. I commented that he had been a United States attorney in New Jersey before becoming a judge and that I thought he was generally an acceptable choice. He resembled Roberts in possessing great intellect and had a longer record of tightly reasoned opinions on the bench to demonstrate it. They were two of the best prospects on the president's short list, if not the two best. Unlike Roberts, who exuded confidence, Alito was shy and retiring in his bearing.

The new nominee's paper trail, however, created a few issues—the most controversial of which was a 1985 job application to Attorney General Ed Meese in which he expressed his pride in contributing to a case "in which the government has argued in the Supreme Court . . . that the Constitution does not protect a right to an abortion." The disclosure of this document by the Ronald Reagan Presidential Library in mid-November provoked the predictable public debate. That was followed by the release of a memorandum the nominee had written at about the same time in the solicitor general's office on the case of *Thornburgh v. American College of Obstetricians and Gynecologists*, suggesting ways to cut back on *Roe*. My immediate reaction was to prevent Alito from falling victim to the prejudgment that short-circuited the Miers nomination in the media. I pointed out that the application and memo had been written over twenty years ago, prior to several subsequent Supreme Court cases that reaffirmed *Roe* under fire, and that people often shift their views over time. This was an area where Yogi Berra's adage applied: "It's hard to make predictions, especially about the future." Justices O'Connor, Kennedy, and Souter all changed their view on *Roe*, if not abortion generally, and the same has been true of several presidents in the three decades since the case was decided.

For me, November 2005 was a milestone month in which I surpassed the record of Boies Penrose, who served in the Senate from 1897 to 1921, as Pennsylvania's longest-serving senator. By Thanksgiving, my hair had all returned, and I was feeling pretty much like my pre-Hodgkin's self, with a few exceptions. My eyes watered intermittently and my libido was not the same, conditions that persisted long after my last chemotherapy treatment. I still could not use regular toothpaste. As for the hair, my friend Lynda Barness once joked after her own experience with breast cancer that chemotherapy gives the patient someone else's hair. Her hair had gone from straight to curly, and the same had happened to Paula Kline. Most seem to go curly after chemotherapy, but my once curly hair grew back almost entirely straight, with a little wave in the front.

Both of my sisters said that I looked more like my father after my treatments than before. My Aunt Rose called me from Wichita to say jubilantly that she was so pleased to see my hair return, she got down on her hands and knees to catch a better view on the television screen. My face became somewhat thinner than it was before chemotherapy, which may have given me a more youthful appearance. Senator Stevens asked if I had had a face-lift. I said no, adding that chemotherapy reportedly changed many of the body's cells, which might account for my face looking thinner.

Hilda attributed the improvement to "the power of spirit," and I enjoyed jokingly comparing myself to Samson, whose strength returned with his hair. Our granddaughter Perri remarked that as my hair returned, "I thought that he was getting better and better from his sickness, and that if he grew all his hair back, then he'd be all better." Many adults seem to have had the same reaction.

The experience of being ill may well have enhanced my political effectiveness. I have come to believe that the sicker you are, the more sympathetic friends you acquire, and this translates into more support politically. When I walked into the well of the Senate every day with less hair and my gaunt appearance, people were friendlier, perhaps because they feared they would not have a chance to be friendly much longer. At the same time, I also learned a lot about myself over the course of the year as I served as chairman. Although I had chaired other committees, none was quite like Judiciary. That experience has taught me more about how to consult with others, how to elicit opinions, how to forge consensus, even how to reconsider. *The Hill*, a newspaper devoted to congressional affairs, ran a complimentary editorial about me in 2006 calling me a "Dealmaker,"[3] not an appellation traditionally associated with me. The following year, I took the opportunity at a Saturday dinner in New York City attended by most Pennsylvania lawmakers, Democrat and Republican, to urge those gathered: "If you can lift a glass together with your colleague from across the aisle on a Saturday night here in New York, you can lift your pen with that same colleague across the hall on Monday morning in Philadelphia, Pittsburgh, Harrisburg, or any place in our state." Previously, I may have been best remembered, to paraphrase my old law partner Mark Klugheit, for believing a theory most people doubted (the single bullet) and doubting a woman most people believed (Anita Hill).[4] The 109th Congress marked a different experience from being the lone ranger, which is not to say my highly prized independence ever left me.

As 2005 reached its end, I became surrounded by other battles to supplement the Alito nomination. The Patriot Act, which contrary to expectation was reported out of the Judiciary Committee unanimously in July, was held up on the Senate floor. I had expected a compromise between Senate and House leaders to pass, but several members modified their agreement to support the compromise. Then on December 16, during the final day of debate over the Patriot Act, *The New York Times* broke a story about a secret program authorized by the president where the National Security Agency (NSA) tapped phone calls without first obtaining a warrant as required by the Foreign Intelligence Surveillance Act (FISA).[5] The president countered that he had inherent authority to conduct the surveillance without prior judicial approval under his Article II powers as commander in chief, which, he argued, trumped the statute. The Judiciary Committee and I have been very heavily involved in this issue, which is in the federal courts.

By late December, I was feeling pretty good, with most of the aftereffects of Hodgkin's gone, so I decided to travel abroad for a break from Alito, which would be all-consuming during January. In Iraq, I met with Judge Rizgar Mohammed Amin, who was presiding over the trial of Saddam Hussein. I asked Judge Rizgar why he allowed Saddam to be so boisterous and disruptive at the trial. He responded that he thought it very important to give every defendant, even Saddam, fairness and due process. I respectfully pointed out that even in the United States, the trial judge can restrain such conduct by gagging the defendant or even putting him out of the courtroom. Judge Rizgar said he thought it preferable to give Saddam the extra leeway. I replied that I understood his rationale and complimented him on taking on such a difficult and dangerous case. A few weeks later, Judge Rizgar resigned from the case.

The hearings for Judge Alito took place the week of January 9 and turned out to be more acrimonious than the Roberts hearings. The nominee was a Princeton graduate, and the most aggressive tactics came from Senator Kennedy, who pursued a long line of questions on his membership in Concerned Alumni of Princeton (CAP), a conservative group of alumni. Before lunch on the second day of questioning, Senator Kennedy showcased articles in CAP's magazine, *Prospect*, that contained disparaging statements about women and minorities. Given the lack of evidence that Alito had any visible role in the group or its magazine, it appeared to be an exercise in assigning guilt by association, with Alito saying at one point, "I disagree with all of that. I would never endorse it. I never have endorsed it. Had I thought that that's what this organization stood for, I would never associate myself with it in any way."[6]

Then Kennedy unexpectedly demanded a subpoena for CAP records held by a founder of CAP, William Rusher, which were located in the Library of Congress. That led to this exchange:

SENATOR KENNEDY: . . . I move that the Committee go into executive session for the purpose of voting on the issuance of the subpoena of those records.

CHAIRMAN SPECTER: We will consider that, Senator Kennedy. There are many, many requests which are coming to me from many quarters. Quite candidly, I view the request, if it is really a matter of importance, you and I see each other all the time. You have never mentioned it to me. I do not ascribe a great deal of weight. We actually didn't get a letter, but—

SENATOR KENNEDY: You did get a letter, are you saying?

CHAIRMAN SPECTER: Well, now wait a minute. You don't know what I got. I am about to—

SENATOR KENNEDY: Of course, I do, Senator, since I sent it.

CHAIRMAN SPECTER: Well, the sender—

SENATOR KENNEDY: I have got it right here.

CHAIRMAN SPECTER: [continuing]. Doesn't necessarily know what the recipient gets, Senator Kennedy.

SENATOR KENNEDY: I have got it right here.

CHAIRMAN SPECTER: You are not in the position to say what I received. If you will bear with me for just one minute—

SENATOR KENNEDY: But I am in a position to say what I sent to you on December 22, so I renew my—

CHAIRMAN SPECTER: You are in a position to tell me what you sent.

SENATOR KENNEDY: I renew my request, Senator, and if I am going to be denied, then I would appeal the decision of the Chair. I think we are entitled to this information. It deals with the fundamental issues of equality and discrimination. This nominee has indicated he has no objection to us seeing these issues. We have gone over the questions and we are entitled to get that kind of information. And if you are going to rule it out of order, I want to have a vote on that here on our Committee.

CHAIRMAN SPECTER: Well, don't be premature, Senator Kennedy. I am not about to make a ruling on this state of the record. I hope you won't mind if I consider it, and I hope you won't mind if I give you the specifics that there was no letter which I received. I take umbrage at your telling me what I received. I don't mind your telling me what you mailed. But there is a big difference between what is mailed and what is received and you know that.[7]

A political cartoon by Chip Bok of the *Akron Beacon-Journal* lampooned the moment with a depiction of Senator Kennedy and me fighting. Kennedy, armed with a broken bottle, was lunging over Leahy to get to me. I had only my gavel. Biden, sitting on the side, had his arm raised in the air as if still midspeech, with a spider web dangling from it. The only dialogue in the cartoon came from Leahy, who asked Alito, "This respect of yours for the legislative branch, judge . . . Where's that come from?"

Over the lunch hour, my chief counsel, Michael O'Neill, contacted Rusher, who immediately gave his permission to have his documents reviewed. The records showed no involvement by Alito. I found it curious that Kennedy did not mention such an important matter to me personally. When the hearing reconvened after lunch, I remarked: "Senator Kennedy and I frequent the gym at the same time and talk all the time, and he never mentioned it to me. . . ."[8] Senator Kennedy responded in part, saying, "I regret I have not been down in the gym since before Christmas so I have missed you down there." People have commented to me frequently about the Roberts and Alito hearings, but this exchange with Senator Kennedy produced by far the most public reaction. I have since recounted this incident by joking that Senator Kennedy has not been in the gym since the Johnson administration—the Andrew Johnson administration.

As it turned out, my staff worked until 2:00 A.M. that night scouring the Rusher papers in the Library of Congress, and found no mention of Alito. Senator Kennedy's tactic may well have been a clumsy attempt to provoke and justify a filibuster by getting a ruling from me denying access to the Rusher files. Either way, it amounted to an act of ill-fated grandstanding that was not well thought out. That episode and the Democrats' questions provoking Martha Alito, the nominee's wife, to burst into tears were probably decisive in derailing the opposition to the nomination. Alito was confirmed by nearly a party-line vote, 58 to 42, on January 31. So ended the seven-month quest to replace Justice O'Connor.

The next thirty days saw the passage of the Patriot Act reauthorization by the surprisingly wide margin of 95 to 4, but that followed a heartbreaking defeat for the asbestos bill on the Senate floor two weeks earlier, when 59 senators voted to waive a procedural issue, one vote short. That setback anticipated the passing of a co-architect of the bill.

While I continued to improve in my battle with Hodgkin's, prostate cancer claimed the life of Judge Becker. I did not wait for his death to deliver his eulogy, but did so on the Senate floor on April 24. Among my comments were the following:

> In addition to his 35-plus years on the Federal bench, he also has the distinction of being the 101st United States Senator. Some, who have laid claim to the position of 101st Senator, have enhanced their status. To identify Judge Becker as the 101st Senator is to enhance the status of the United States Senate.
>
> Judge Becker became a member of the Senate's family by his negotiating, cajoling, and writing most of Senate Bill 852 dealing with asbestos reform. . . .
>
> When appointed to the Federal Bench in 1970 at the age of 37, he merited the position both in terms of exceptional competency and extraordinary contribution to his party. No one in my experience has merited the

appointment to the Federal bench more than Judge Becker on both counts. . . .

Among his landmark decisions are three opinions adopted by the Supreme Court on cutting-edge issues. . . . He was consistently recognized by the University of Chicago Law Review as being among the three Circuit Judges most often cited by the Supreme Court. . . .

When I was diagnosed with Hodgkin's last year, I followed his advice on how to cope. He was an inspiration and model to me.

Watching close friends suffer and die from cancer, and from my own experience with Hodgkin's, all of that has reinforced my determination to work to secure sufficient funding for the National Institutes of Health to conquer cancer and other maladies. . . .

Visiting Judge Becker at his home last Saturday, I saw a large stack of briefs on his desk and observed him carrying on his judicial duties from his living room with determination and gusto, notwithstanding his prostate cancer. From my own experience with Hodgkin's, I know cancer can be beaten. From watching Judge Becker, I have seen him beat cancer for more than 3 years.

My statement today has the dual purpose, No. 1, of recognizing and acknowledging the public service and contributions of a truly great American, and, No. 2, urging my Senate colleagues who have come to know, admire, and respect Judge Becker to support adequate funding to win the war against cancer.[9]

After Ed read my speech, memorialized in the *Congressional Record*, he called me. Choosing his words very carefully, he said, "I will be eternally grateful." On May 19, as I was chairing a hearing on campus crime, a member of my staff entered the hearing room and handed me a note with the bad news: Ed had just died. I had spoken with him about the ongoing battle to advance cancer research in our last conversation that morning.

When Steve Harmelin spoke at Ed's funeral, he expressed his surprise when he first heard that I wanted to get Ed involved in the asbestos legislation when he was so sick. Steve thought, "How could he do that?" But then, after a moment, he thought further: "How could he not? Because that's what Arlen would do: Work even harder." Steve may have been correct, but our friend's death stood as a sobering reminder that sometimes even one's best efforts are not enough to overcome a serious illness.

Ed Becker's death intensified my efforts to get additional funding for the NIH and cancer research. When the Appropriations Committee approved cuts in that funding, I cast the sole dissenting vote on the 2006 supplementary appropriation bill, which passed the Senate 99 to 1. Presenting the subcommittee bill to the full Appropriations Committee at its markup, I decried the inadequate funding, asserting, "This bill represents the disintegration of the appropriate federal role in health." There is no more important frontier for the government to explore than our health.

On the Judiciary front, there remained plenty of matters on my plate, and I was glad to find myself in the middle of them—sometimes ideologically as well as institutionally. I employed the chairmanship repeatedly to decry an inert Congress that failed to stand up to the president and exercise effective oversight. That pleased the Bush administration's critics. After such oversight occurred and we collected further information about the executive branch's surveillance activities, I negotiated with the president on legislation that would strike a balance between our national security needs and the need for proper checks and balances. It made some administration critics incredulous that I would dare reach a consensus with the administration. On a related front, it was gratifying to see that after leaving the matter to the courts for five years, Congress in late 2006 enacted legislation governing the military tribunals with jurisdiction over those detained during the war on terror.

When all was said and done, much of the Senate's work during the 109th Congress had come through the Judiciary Committee: a new attorney general, class-action lawsuit reform, bankruptcy reform, the confirmation of previously filibustered judges, two new additions to the Supreme Court, the Patriot Act reauthorization, the renewal of the Voting Rights Act, a security fence on the border, and legislation on war crimes trials. The level of activity on the committee prompted Senator Lott to say to me, "Cool your burners." With the business of the 110th Congress on the horizon, I looked forward to moving forward on issues where work remains to be done: immigration, crime control, oil prices, the insurance company antitrust exemption, the reporters' privilege, identity theft, and asbestos litigation reform.

In addition to committee work, I took the opportunity during the year following my recovery from treatment to speak out on the floor about our policy with respect to international hot spots like Iran and North Korea, and to travel to parts of the world I could visit in South America, Europe, Asia, the Middle East, and North Africa. While in Peru in April, I visited the city of Cuzco in the Andes Mountains. The city stands eleven thousand feet high, which made Captain Ron Smith, who accompanied me on many of my trips, apprehensive, given my medical history. A colleague of his with a heart condition had died in his forties at a high elevation. As it turned out, I felt fine. I later visited the Incan ruins at Machu Picchu at nearly eight thousand feet. During my August trip, which took me to several destinations from China to Libya, I ventured into an eleven-thousand-foot area in the mountain kingdom of Bhutan.

During my August travels, I made a stop at a women's center in Nepal with Joan and Chris Bradish, a staff member who assists me on issues of foreign policy, defense, and trade. The center, which was funded in part by the United States Agency for International Development (USAID), was dedicated to assisting the girls and young women who were victims or at high risk of being victims of human sex trafficking. I made an appearance to unveil a motorbike that would be used to help them with their occupational training. In a spontaneous moment, I whisked off the red sheet that covered the vehicle like a toreador waving his flag before the bull. The assembled crowd, enjoying the moment with me, cheered, with smiles from ear to ear as I raised my hands. I then mounted the motorbike, gripping both handles with what Chris Bradish described as a boyish grin on my face as he snapped my picture. It had been a while since he last saw that grin—election night 2004 to be precise, at the moment I joined my victory party with a martini in each hand. Seeing that expression again, he thought to himself, *It's official: We're back!*

Concluding Thoughts

W HEN FACING THE life-threatening challenge of Hodgkin's, I found strength in my experience in surmounting my 1979 diagnosis of ALS, beating the brain tumor in 1993 and its recurrence in 1996, and recovering from serious problems following heart bypass surgery in 1998. I thought frequently about Winston Churchill's statement after surviving combat in the North-West Frontier of British India: "Nothing in life is so exhilarating as to be shot at without result."[1]

I also drew strength from reminiscing about so many difficult challenges and succeeding: winning the first conviction of the Teamsters Union officials after the McClellan Committee's corruption investigation; developing the single-bullet theory for the Warren Commission; beating the entrenched Philadelphia Democratic machine for district attorney; winning a Pennsylvania statewide Republican primary after three tries; withstanding controversial positions taken in the Bork and Thomas confirmation hearings, including reelection in 1992 after questioning Professor Anita Hill; winning a brutal Republican primary election in 2004; setting the record as Pennsylvania's longest-serving senator after winning five elections.

Looking back at my illness, President Bush remarked, "The best way I can determine whether or not someone can whip disease is their attitude. The first stage toward whipping disease—some diseases—is whether or not the patient is a battler. And you know, this story has to be one of Arlen Specter the battler." He added, "Had I not known him, I would've said . . . I'm surprised" in reference to my ability to maintain my Senate duties. The President continued, "When you look into a man's eyes, and you hear his voice and his determination, then in retrospect, I wasn't surprised."

Neil Oxman, a political consultant who has represented my opponents, remarked in 2006, "When I think of Arlen, I think of those horror movies where you think the guy is dead and in the coffin, and then the last scene is a shot of a hand coming up through the casket. That's Arlen's political career."[2]

Professionally, I have demonstrated a pattern of swimming upstream—an exhilarating experience. The tougher the battle, the sweeter the victory. The key factor is to keep working and keep fighting. When I became ill with Hodgkin's in early 2005, I was lucky to have such demanding work to take my mind off my illness: the confirmation of Attorney General Alberto Gonzales; the detainees at Guantánamo; reauthorization of the Voting Rights Act and the Patriot Act; dealing with the explosive presidential directive on electronic surveillance; reform legislation on immigration, asbestos litigation, bankruptcy, and class actions; the pitched battle on federal judges involving the Democrats' filibuster and the Republican proposal of the constitutional/nuclear option; and the confirmations of Chief Justice John Roberts and Justice Samuel Alito.

People ask me what my legacy will be, and I respond that it is far too early in my career to give an answer. The Senate will give me the continuing opportunity to contribute and figure out the legacy answer.

Through a tumultuous 2005 and 2006 recovering from Hodgkin's and chemotherapy, I gained a new passion for life. As a child, I saw Lionel Barrymore star in the movie *On Borrowed Time*. In it a grandfather somehow manages to confine a character named Mr. Brink, the personification of death, to the top of an old apple tree so that he has extra time to resolve issues about the future of his orphaned grandson. I now think of myself as living on borrowed time. It was not always that way. I have gone through life as conscious as anyone that our days are numbered. In my mind, the passage of each day would mark one less day I have to live. The experience of becoming seriously ill with what could be a fatal disease changes this perspective. All of a sudden, every day is an unexpected day, a bonus. Every day is a great gift, a precious jewel.

Immediately upon election to the Senate in 1980, I

chose to serve on the Appropriations Subcommittee for Labor, Health and Human Services, and Education. I knew that good health was a person's most important possession. I had played squash virtually every day for a decade. I watched my diet under the close surveillance of my gourmet, calorie-conscious wife. I observed her rule never to eat standing up—an easy way to lose track of what you consume—while attending Washington's continuous receptions, which made growing fat an occupational hazard.

In my subcommittee work, having observed the tremendous potential of medical research by the NIH to conquer virtually all maladies, I joined with Senator Harkin to more than double NIH funding. The Specter-Harkin bill to authorize federal funding for embryonic stem-cell research, however, was vetoed by President Bush in 2006 after being passed by both houses.

I truly believe if the war on cancer declared in 1970 had been pursued with the same intensity we apply to other wars, it is likely cancer would have been conquered; Judge Becker would not have died of prostate cancer; Carey Lackman and Paula Kline would not have died of breast cancer; and I would not have contracted Hodgkin's. Thousands of lives would have been saved. My primary goal in the Senate will continue to be to promote a national passion for life and to provide adequate funding to conquer cancer and other medical maladies.

Only recently have I understood some of the ways in which my career in public life has touched people. Chris Picaut of the attending physician's office reported that he did not recall receiving a single call about the gamma knife before it was used on me. Afterward, he received three to four calls per week inquiring about it, something I learned only a decade later. He also reported how concerned the many military medical personnel were as I struggled with Hodgkin's so that I would survive to continue my work on the Veterans Committee. Carrie Stricker, the nurse who helped me during chemotherapy, never mentioned to me during treatment that her best friend died on Flight 93, the plane that crashed in Shanksville, Pennsylvania, on September 11, 2001, as the heroism of the passengers kept the plane from its probable target, the U.S. Capitol. Only later did she tell me about the impact of my work to establish a memorial to the Flight 93 victims. I have more people to thank than will ever have me to thank.

It has been very gratifying to have met and heard from so many people suffering from cancer who have been encouraged by my fight against Hodgkin's. During a September 2006 political rally, a Pennsylvania constituent, Judith C. Strimmel, told me she was advised to come back in six months after a breast cancer checkup. Instead, after seeing me discuss my situation on television, she immediately saw another doctor, who told her that a six-month wait would have killed her. Joan recently told her high school classmate, Harriet Part, whose husband was just diagnosed with non-Hodgkin's lymphoma, that I was writing about my experience with cancer. At Harriet's request, I sent her my preliminary manuscript. Harriet reported that her husband, who had been listless, fatigued, and staying in bed, read my report and said, "If Arlen can do it, so can I." For the first time, he left the house to walk the dog.

The visibility of my position in the Senate has publicized my story. I reacted instinctively to minimize the pain of Hodgkin's. My sense of purpose has given me the greatest therapy to fight and beat cancer. I hope others in every walk of life will consider my experience. For whatever it is worth, I pass along this advice to those who face a challenge to their health:

1. Acknowledge the basic fact with respect to your illness that "whatever is, is" and move on from there.
2. Organize and focus on as much of your psychological strength as you can muster to face your medical problems. There are obviously limits to what a person can physiologically or mentally sustain, but you can surprise yourself as to how far you can go on sheer tenacity.
3. As much as possible, maintain your regular work and exercise schedule without succumbing to pain and other distractions from your fitness goals.
4. Supplement your doctor's advice by learning as much as you can about your medical conditions so that you are equipped to question, even challenge, the expert medical professionals. To this end, seek second opinions whenever you can, and make sure

you have cast a net wide enough to get the best available professional help.

5. Listen to your body, because your body, in many ways, knows more than your doctors.

6. Keep busy. Follow Churchill's advice: Never, never, never give in!

Note About the National Institutes of Health

I N VARYING WAYS, the National Institutes of Health (NIH) is a 24-hour resource for science-based health information. NIH Institutes and Centers (ICs) provide phone, mail, e-mail, and Web information to the general public, medical professionals, advocacy organizations, and research institutions worldwide. The National Library of Medicine (NLM) is accessible 24 hours a day, 7 days a week via "Ask Cosmo," a Web site response service that links the public to requested information via wwwns.nlm .nih.gov. A toll-free number is also available: 1-888-346-3656.

Many ICs have subject-specific clearinghouses that respond to telephone requests through toll-free numbers and provide information and printed or Web materials. NIH physicians are available around the clock for consultations with medical professionals. Through its communications offices and information clearinghouses, the NIH annually sends out nearly thirty million science-based publications to requestors who rely on the NIH and its news stories, press releases, and publications for authoritative information about the latest research developments.

The National Cancer Institute's (NCI) Cancer Information Service provides the latest, most accurate information about cancer treatment, clinical trials, and early detection and prevention for cancer patients, their families, and the public. U.S. residents may call toll-free at 1-800-4-CANCER (1-800-422-6237). NCI information specialists answer calls in English or Spanish from 9:00 A.M. to 4:30 P.M. Eastern time.

An instant-messaging service called LiveHelp is also available on NCI's Web site at www.cancer.gov. LiveHelp is available in English from 9:00 A.M. to 11:00 P.M. Eastern time. The NCI Web site currently averages 3,065,672 visits per month, accounting for 15,001,742 page views per month. In April 2007, NCI launched the Spanish-language version of this site. Many ICs provide targeted language materials and resources for those with literacy challenges.

The majority of Americans who request NIH information not only use it, but share the materials. More than 40 percent of patients are now bringing materials from the Web with them to discuss with their physician.

NOTES

CHAPTER 1: THE CHALLENGE BEFORE THE CHALLENGE

1. "Does Stress Cause Cancer? Probably Not, Research Finds," *New York Times,* Nov. 29, 2005, F1.

2. Arlen Specter, *Passion for Truth* (New York: Morrow, 2000), 315. Hereafter cited as *PFT.*

3. *PFT,* 274.

4. "GOP's Philosophical Rift Evident in Pennsylvania," *Los Angeles Times,* Apr. 18, 2004, A1.

5. Al Hunt, "Down and Nasty in the Keystone State," *Wall Street Journal,* Apr. 15, 2004, A16.

6. According to FEC data compiled by the Center for Responsive Politics. See "The Battle Hymn of the Republicans," *Pittsburgh City Paper,* Apr. 8, 2004, 19.

7. "Changing Tack in the Winds of Politics; Critics Accuse Specter of Tilting to Right to Thwart Challenge to Senator's Reelection," *Washington Post,* May 18, 2003, A6.

8. "Toomey, Specter May Fight for Same Bucks," *Allentown Morning Call*, Feb. 24, 2003, B1.

9. "Specter's Woes Start with Self," *Philadelphia Inquirer*, Apr. 11, 2004, B01.

10. "Remarks by the President in a Conversation on Homeownership," Main Line YMCA, Ardmore, Pa., Mar. 15, 2004.

11. "President Discusses Education and Changing Job Market," Central Dauphin High School, Harrisburg, Pa., Feb. 12, 2004.

12. "Specter's Power on Display; Senator's Valley Visit Shows Off the Clout of Incumbency," *Allentown Morning Call*, Feb. 18, 2004, A1.

13. *PFT*, 360.

14. *National Review*, Sep. 1, 2003, cover.

15. *Wall Street Journal*, Apr. 15, 2004, A16.

16. John Fund, "Has He Snarled His Last?," *Wall Street Journal*, Apr. 26, 2004.

17. "Specter, Toomey in Spending Spat: Challenges Fly in Bitter Battle for Republican Senate Nomination," *Allentown Morning Call*, Apr. 23, 2004, A1.

18. "Down and Nasty in the Keystone State," *Wall Street Journal*, Apr. 15, 2004, A16.

19. "Bruised and Battered?," *Roll Call*, Mar. 25, 2004.

20. "Poll Shows Toomey Surging as GOP Senate Primary Nears," Associated Press, Apr. 21, 2004.

Notes

Chapter 2: The Autumn of My Career

1. See generally "Hoeffel, Specter in Sharp Contrast on Iraq Policies," *Philadelphia Inquirer,* Oct. 20, 2004, A1.

2. "Specter Wins Fifth Term After Tough Year," Associated Press, Nov. 3, 2004.

3. "All Circuits Are Busy, Sen. Specter," *The Hill,* Nov. 18, 2004, 8.

4. "Specter Seeks, Gets Support," *Washington Post,* Nov. 17, 2004, A8.

5. "Frist Says Specter Hasn't Yet Made Case," *Philadelphia Inquirer,* Nov. 15, 2004, A02.

6. "Republican Opponents Ramp Up Efforts to Deny Arlen Specter the Chairmanship of the Senate Judiciary Committee," *CBS Evening News,* Nov. 16, 2004.

7. "Verbatim," *Roll Call,* Nov. 22, 2004.

8. *CQ Transcriptions,* "U.S. Senators Orrin Hatch and Arlen Specter Hold a News Conference," Nov. 18, 2004.

Chapter 3: An Unwanted Birthday Present

1. *PFT,* 276.

2. *PFT,* 281.

3. Senator Bernie Sanders, who took office in 2007, would represent Vermont as an independent socialist.

4. *PFT,* 531–32.

5. "Senate Confirms Gonzales, 60 to 36," *Washington Post,* Feb. 4, 2005, A01.

6. *PFT,* 474.

Chapter 4: My Health Odyssey

1. "Specter's Tumor Wasn't Cancerous, Faculties Intact," *Pittsburgh Post-Gazette,* Jun. 16, 1993, A1.

2. *PFT,* 432–33.

3. *PFT,* 428–29.

4. "Specter Undergoes Brain Treatment," *Philadelphia Inquirer,* Oct. 12, 1996, B1.

5. *PFT,* 431.

6. *PFT,* 444.

7. *PFT,* 431.

Chapter 5: Facing Treatment, But Not Alone

1. "Sen. Arlen Specter Receives Diagnosis of Hodgkin's Disease," *USA Today,* Feb. 17, 2005, 8A.

2. "Specter Diagnosed with Hodgkin's Disease," Newhouse News Service, Feb. 16, 2005.

3. "The Full Specter," *Philadelphia Magazine,* Nov. 2006, 154.

4. Editorial, *Pittsburgh Post-Gazette,* Feb. 20, 2005, J6.

5. Editorial, *Philadelphia Daily News,* Feb. 23, 2005, 15.

6. "Can't Tell a Lie—Not All Pols Are Presidential," *Philadelphia Daily News,* Feb. 21, 2005, 15.

7. *PFT,* 541.

8. "Upbeat Arlen Says He'll Whip Cancer," *Philadelphia Daily News,* Feb. 19, 2005, 5.

9. "Specter Is Upbeat After Treatment," *Philadelphia Inquirer,* Feb. 19, 2005, B1.

10. *PFT,* 44.

CHAPTER 6: THE BEST THERAPY

1. Alfred Henry Lewis, ed., *A Compilation of the Messages and Speeches of Theodore Roosevelt, 1901–1905* (Bureau of National Literature and Art, 1906), 503.

2. *PFT,* 150.

3. Bill Bradley, *Time Present, Time Past* (New York: Knopf, 1996), 87–88.

4. Federal News Service, Press Conference with Senate Judiciary Chairman Senator Arlen Specter, Feb. 24, 2005.

5. "Specter Is Upbeat After Treatment," *Philadelphia Inquirer,* Feb. 19, 2005, B01.

6. "Bush Tries Again on Court Choices Stalled in Senate," *New York Times,* Dec. 24, 2004, 1.

7. Ibid.

8. Dana Milbank, "Unrepentant Specter Is Finding Life Lonely in the Center," *Washington Post,* Feb. 25, 2005, A04.

9. CNN Late Edition with Wolf Blitzer, Feb. 27, 2005.

10. "Very Much Alive, Thank You," *New York Times,* Jul. 17, 2005, section 4, p. 3.

11. "Cancer Patients Staying at Work," *Philadelphia Inquirer,* Apr. 1, 2005, A1.

12. "Specter's Moment Has Now Arrived," *Pittsburgh Post-Gazette,* Jun. 23, 2005, A1.

13. Despite His Cancer, Arlen Is Still Arlen," *Philadelphia Daily News,* May 4, 2005, 8.

14. *PFT,* 164.

15. 151 Cong. Rec. S4050–S4051 (Apr. 21, 2005).

16. 151 Cong. Rec. S4052 (Apr. 21, 2005).

17. These senators were Robert Byrd (D-WV), Daniel Inouye (D-HI), John Warner (R-VA), John McCain (R-AZ), Joe Lieberman (D-CT), Mike DeWine (R-OH), Olympia Snowe (R-ME), Susan Collins (R-ME), Mary Landrieu (D-LA), Lincoln Chafee (R-RI), Ben Nelson (D-NE), Lindsey Graham (R-SC), Mark Pryor (D-AR), and Ken Salazar (D-CO).

18. "Confirmation Battle in Senate Could Define Specter's Career," *New York Times,* Jul. 3, 2005, 1.

19. "Biden Unwraps His Bid for '08 with an Oops!," *New York Times,* Feb. 1, 2007, A1.

20. CQ Transcriptions, U.S. Senator Arlen Specter Holds Markup Hearing on FAIR Act, May 26, 2005.

21. David Johnston, "Leak Revelation Leaves Questions," *New York Times,* Sept. 2, 2006, A1.

Chapter 7: Seeking Cures for Others

1. *PFT*, 534.

2. Hearing before a Subcommittee of the Committee on Appropriations, United States Senate, 109th Congress, 1st Session, Special Hearing, Johanna's Law, May 11, 2005, 7–8.

3. NIH Hearing Transcript, Apr. 6, 2005, 177–78.

4. Ibid., 179.

5. "Stem Cells May Be Key to Cancer," *New York Times,* Feb. 2, 2006, D1.

6. See "Embryo Adoption on Increase; Donors Help Other Infertile Couples Build Families," *Washington Times,* Nov. 29, 2006, A3.

7. ABC News Transcripts, *This Week with George Stephanopoulos,* May 29, 2005.

8. CBS News Transcripts, *CBS Evening News,* June 3, 2005.

9. ABC News Transcripts, *World News Tonight with Peter Jennings,* July 25, 2005.

10. Gina Kolata, "Scientists Bypass Need for Embryo to Get Stem Cells," *New York Times,* Nov. 21, 2007, p. A1.

Chapter 8: Playing for the Ages

1. Federal News Service, Press Conference with Senator Arlen Specter, Chairman of the Senate Judiciary Committee, July 1, 2005.

2. "Specter Is 'Ready' for Court Nominee," *Baltimore Sun,* Jul. 5, 2005, 1A.

3. NBC News Transcripts, *Meet the Press,* July 3, 2005.

4. *Pittsburgh Post-Gazette,* Jul. 19, 2004, A1.

5. See *Board of Trustees of the University of Alabama v. Garrett,* 531 U.S. 356 (2001); *Tennessee v. Lane,* 541 U.S. 509 (2004).

6. Sheryl Gay Stolberg, "Abortion Rights Group Plans to Pull Ad on Roberts," *New York Times,* Aug. 12, 2005, A1.

7. *PFT,* 303.

8. *The NewsHour with Jim Lehrer,* Aug. 24, 2005.

9. *CNN American Morning,* Sept. 12, 2005.

10. *PFT,* 545.

11. *PFT,* 310.

12. Committee on the Judiciary, United States Senate, Confirmation Hearing on the Nomination of John G. Roberts Jr. to be Chief Justice of the United States, 109th Congress, 1st Session, Sept. 12–15, 2005, 193.

13. Ibid., 283.

14. Ibid., 387.

15. Ibid., 324.

16. "Right Pleased with Specter; Approach to Roberts Praised," *Roll Call,* Sep. 13, 2005.

17. "Specter Rises Above 2004 'Worst Republican' Title," *Washington Times,* Sep. 5, 2005.

CHAPTER 9: THE MISSION CONTINUES

1. "Senators in G.O.P. Voice New Doubt on Court Choice," *New York Times,* Oct. 26, 2006, A1.

2. *Washington Post,* Nov. 4, 2005, A7.

3. "Dealmaker," *The Hill,* May 17, 2006, 26.

4. *PFT,* 4.

5. "Bush Lets U.S. Spy on Callers Without Courts," Dec. 16, 2005, A1.

6. Committee on the Judiciary, United States Senate, Confirmation Hearing on the Nomination of Samuel A. Alito, Jr. to be an Associate Justice of the Supreme Court of the United States, 109th Congress, 2nd session, Jan. 9–13, 2006, 496.

7. Ibid., 498–499.

8. Ibid., 522.

9. 152 Cong. Rec. S3428–S3429, 109th Congress, 2nd Session, Apr. 24, 2006.

CONCLUDING THOUGHTS

1. Winston S. Churchill, *The Story of the Malakand Field Force,* (Kessinger Publishing, 2004).

2. "The Full Specter," *Philadelphia Magazine,* Nov. 2006, 154.

3. *Abrams v. United States,* 250 U.S. 616, 630 (1919) (Holmes, J., dissenting).

4. Roy P. Basler, ed., *Abraham Lincoln: His Speeches and Writings* (Cleveland: World, 1946), 504.

INDEX

Index

Index

Index

Freind, Steve, 14
Frist, Bill, 25, 52–53, 55, 115, 162–63,
    194–95, 199, 200, 224

gamma knife, 95–97, 247
Gang of Fourteen, 163, 165
Garth, David, 131–32
Gehrig, Lou, 179
general elections, 1, 33, 36
Georgetown Law Center, 204
Georgetown University Hospital, 31
Gleason, Andy, 151
Glick, John H., 79–86, 93, 102, 109,
    111–13, 122–24, 139, 149–50, 153–55,
    180, 205, 207
Gola, Tom, 12
Gonzales, Alberto, 67–71, 75–77, 245
Graham, Lindsey, 44, 47, 137, 168
Grassley, Chuck, 49, 56, 168
Greenberg, Danny, 22
Gregg, Judd, 47, 53
Guantanamo Bay, 170, 207–8, 246

Haabestad, Harold "Bud," 10
hair loss, 83–84, 146–47, 158–59, 164–65,
    214, 218, 230–31
Har Zion Temple, 132
Harkin, Tom, 110, 155, 174, 181,
    183–84, 247
Harmelin, Julia, 125, 127
Harmelin, Steve, 29, 33–34, 125–26,
    128, 240
Hart, Gary, 71
Harvey, Tom, 129
Hatch, Orrin, 13, 47, 54, 56–58, 66, 71,
    114, 183–84
    as "Iron Pants," 68
Hatfield, Mark, 9
Hayakawa, Sam, 76
Hearn, Gail, 128
Hearn, Peter, 128, 158
heart disease, 97–101, 174, 182, 210
Heinz, John, 9, 10, 12, 108, 131–32
Henry, Ed, 214–15
hernia, 60
Herrero, Rolando, 209
Hilda (sister), 22, 119, 231
Hill, Anita, 8, 199, 232, 245
Hitler, Adolf, 173
Hodgkin's disease. See Hodgkin's lymphoma
Hodgkin's lymphoma, 2, 9, 81–86, 93–94,
    112–13, 122–25, 137, 149, 173–74,
    176, 181, 196, 205, 210, 239, 244–49
    stages of, 82, 85, 112
Hoeffel, Joe, 34–35
Hollings, Fritz, 120
Holmes, Oliver Wendell, xiii, 250

Hospital of the University of Pennsylvania
    (HUP), 84, 87, 90, 111, 113, 122,
    171, 205
House of Representatives, 183
    Energy and Commerce Committee, 6
Howard, Marc, 100–101
HPV. See human papiloma virus
human papiloma virus (HPV), 209
Hunt, Al, 25
HUP. See Hospital of the University of
    Pennsylvania
Hurricane Katrina, 210–11, 212
Hussein, Saddam, 35–36, 173, 233
Hutchison, Kay Bailey, 50
Hutson, John, 70

identity theft, 158, 241
Ifill, Gwen, 210
immigration issues, 68, 241, 246
immigration reform, 210
immune system, 4–5
impeachment, 162
insurance company antitrust
    exemption, 241
intellectual property rights, 68
interrogation, 69
intestinal cancer, 5
Iraq, 61
    provisional government in, 36
    war in, 35, 183
"Iron Pants," 68
Israel, 14

Jackson, Henry "Scoop," 63
Jackson, Jesse, 166
Jackson, Robert H., 36
Javits, Jacob, 23
Jefferson Hospital. See Thomas Jefferson
    University Hospital
Jeffords, Jim, 142, 220
Jennings, Peter, 176
Jensen, Peter, 82
Jewish tradition, 51, 119, 132
Johanna's Law, 177–78
John Paul II (pope), 175
John, Tommy, 179
Johns Hopkins Hospital, 94
Johnson, Andrew, 162, 237
Johnson, Douglas, 70
Johnson, Lyndon B., 151
Judiciary Committee, 8, 16, 40–41, 77,
    114–15, 157, 188, 195, 210
    chairmanship of, 1, 13, 37, 43–44, 46,
    49, 53–58, 232, 240–41
    confirmation hearings by, 67–70, 228
    judicial nominations and, 138–40, 160,
    200, 222, 226

Index

NSA. *See* National Security Agency
"nuclear option," 143–44, 160–63, 191, 246

Obama, Barack, 166
O'Connor, John, 190
O'Connor, Sandra Day, 38, 40, 190–91,
    193–96, 211, 222–24, 230, 238
oil prices, 241
On Borrowed Time, 246
O'Neill, Michael, 82, 221, 237, 240
organized crime, 68
Ornish, Dean, 154
osteoporosis, 179
ovarian cancer, 177
Oxman, Neil, 245

Packwood, Bob, 9
Paez, Richard, 142
pancreatic cancer, 5
Parkinson's disease, 175, 180, 182
Part, Harriet, 248
Passion for Truth (Specter), 2, 68, 118
Paterno, Joe, 156–57, 187
Patriot Act, 69, 171, 200, 232–33, 238,
    241, 246
Penrose, Boies, 230
People for the American Way, 199
Percy, Charles, 9
PET. *See* Positron Emission Tomography
Philadelphia, 7–8
Philadelphia Naval Shipyard, 91
Picaut, Chris, 156, 247
"pink sisters," 28
Planned Parenthood v. Casey, 38
pluripotent stem cell technology, 188–89
"pork," 25–26. *See also* federal projects
positive mental attitude, 83
Positron Emission Tomography (PET), 82,
    85, 112, 149, 171, 205
Powell, Lewis, 225
prednisone, 121
presidential elections, 36–37, 92
presidential nominations, 16, 64–65, 82,
    139–44, 160–61, 226, 241, 246
primary elections, 1, 8, 10, 12, 28, 58
pro-choice, 14, 43, 50, 206
Profiles in Courage (Kennedy), 162
pro-life, 14–15, 38, 42, 54, 183
prostate cancer, 72, 74, 147, 238

al Qaeda, 170

Rayburn, Sam, 155
Reagan, Nancy, 187
Reagan, Ronald, 141–42, 194
    Presidential Library, 230
Reed-Sternberg cells, 81

Rehnquist, William H., 40, 75, 176, 190,
    211, 213, 220
Reid, Harry, 53, 162–63, 194, 224–25
Religious Freedom Restoration Act, 203
religious right, 49
Rendell, Ed, 27, 116–17, 158
Rendell, Marjorie, 117
Reno, Janet, 101–2
reporter's privilege, 200, 241
Republican Conference Rules, 37
Republican party, 30–31, 73
    candidates, 8
    incumbents, 9–10
    primary elections, 1, 8, 10, 12, 28
    Specter, Arlen, in, 7–8
Republican Senatorial Campaign
    Committee, 42
Reynolds, Bill, 211
Ridge, Tom, 10
Rivers, Joan, 179
Robbins, Charlie, 27, 41
Roberts, John, 197–200, 204, 206–7,
    210–17, 219, 222, 223, 225, 229, 234,
    237, 246
Roberts, Pat, 47, 218
Robertson, Pat, 49
Rocky, 36
Roe v. Wade, 14–15, 38, 40–41, 223, 230
Rogers, Roy, 177
Roll Call, 27
Ronald Reagan Presidential Library, 230
Roosevelt, Franklin D., 65
Roosevelt, Theodore, 134
Rose (aunt), 22–23, 160–61, 231
Rosen, Ed, 128
Rosen, Evelyn, 128
Rove, Karl, 48–49, 187, 195–96, 198
Rudman, Warren, 9
Rusher, William, 234, 237
Rushton, Sean, 199, 220
Russell Rotunda, 76
Rybka, Witold, 116

Samson, 231
Santorum, Rick, 15, 39, 48–49, 110, 138,
    184, 187–88, 195
Santorum-Specter bill, 189
Sarokin, H. Lee, 142
Saturday Night Massacre, 8
sayings
    amendments, 166
    be shot at, 244
    death, 87
    experience, 87
    give 60 percent, 216
    good/bad/better, 170
    know what you say, 59

Index

man/God, 211
never give in, 106, 250
predictions, 230
slogans, 12
step softly, 52
this, too, 250
time and faith, 250
work hard, 134
Scalia, Antonin, 223
Schilling, Curt, 98
Schumer, Chuck, 140, 144–45, 218, 225
security fence, 241
Senate, 31
Appropriations Committee, 11, 24, 78,
80, 110, 138, 173, 240, 246
bills, 64
committee procedures, 64–65
"constitutional option," 143–44, 160–63,
191, 246
debate in, 64
Finance Committee, 40
Foreign Relations Committee, 64
Judiciary Committee, 1, 8, 13, 16, 37,
40–41, 43–44, 46, 49, 53–58, 62–66,
67–70, 77, 114–15, 138–40, 157, 160,
188, 195, 200, 210, 222, 226, 228, 232,
233, 240–41
"nuclear option," 143–44, 160–63,
191, 246
Veterans Affairs Committee, 24
workweek, 172
Senate Republican Conference, 37,
45, 115
September 11, 2001, terrorist attacks, 68,
207, 248
Sessions, Jeff, 50
700 Club, 49
sexual abstinence programs, 14
Shanin, Freda (grandmother), 211
Sharpton, Al, 166
Shirley (sister), 22, 119
Short, Carolyn, 61, 77
Simpson, Alan, 9
Sinatra, Frank, 153
skin lesion, 66
Slaiman, Gary, 169
Slease, Terry, 120
Smerconish, Michael, 19
Smith, Bob, 9
Smith, Gordon, 10, 183–84
Smith, Ron, 242
Snowe, Olympia, 10
Snyder, Allen, 199
Souter, David, 39, 230
Specter, Arlen
in Air Force, 7, 73
atrial fibrillation and, 97

autobiography, 2
background of, 17, 22–23, 62, 73
brain tumor and, 2, 89–92, 210, 244
burial plans of, 51
campaign slogans of, 12
campaigning with Bush, George W.,
15–16, 79
Democratic party and, 21–22, 131
as district attorney, 7–8, 12, 21,
65–66, 244
early Senate years, 63
as "Enabler in Chief," 34
gubernatorial run, 8
hair loss and, 83–84, 146–47, 158–59,
164–65, 214, 218, 230–31
heart disease and, 97–101, 210
hernia and, 60
Hodgkin's lymphoma and, 2, 9, 81–86,
93–94, 112–13, 122–25, 149, 173–74,
181, 196, 205, 239, 244–49
as Judiciary Committee chairman, 1,
56–57, 62, 66–68, 114, 163–64, 170,
173, 198, 215, 220, 230–41, 232
as longest-serving senator, 230, 245
mayoral run, 8, 30, 125
meningioma and, 92
presidential run, 49
Republican party and, 7–8
Senate run 1980, 8, 10, 245
Senate run 1986, 11
Senate run 1992, 11, 14,
33, 245
Senate run 1998, 11, 102
Senate run 2004, 10–11, 16–19, 25–32,
33, 36–37, 245
Watch, 34
"wins ugly," 26–27
Specter, Avram (grandfather), 22
Specter, Harry (father), 59, 129–31,
134–35, 216
Specter, Hatti (granddaughter), 79,
153, 158
Specter, Joan Levy (wife), 20,
28, 30, 39, 51–52, 73, 74,
77, 80, 84–85, 88–93, 99–100, 127–29,
132–33, 153,
197, 198, 242
Specter, Lilli (granddaughter), 79, 118,
153, 158
Specter, Lilli Shanin (mother), 118
Specter, Morton (brother), 135
Specter, Perri (granddaughter), 20, 67, 79,
97, 119, 158, 198, 231
Specter, Shanin (son), 17, 20–21, 28, 30,
50, 51, 55–56, 59–60, 77, 79, 80, 84,
91–93, 100–101, 108, 111, 132–33,
135, 169, 204

Index

Specter, Silvi (granddaughter), 20, 21, 77, 79, 97, 118–19, 153
Specter, Steve (son), 21–22, 93, 133, 135
Specter, Tracey (daughter-in-law), 20, 28, 51, 77, 79, 133, 169, 204
Specter-Harkin bill, 188, 247
"Specterpalooza," 19
squash (game), 18, 102–5, 113, 117, 139, 150, 193, 204, 246
Stafford, Bob, 9
stare decisis, 38, 203
State of the Union addresses, 76
Stein, Jay M., 132
stem cell research, 14, 43, 181–89, 195, 200, 204, 247
Stevens, Ted, 231
Stolberg, Sheryl Gay, 163
Stone, Roger, 49
stress and cancer, 4, 9, 33, 60, 70, 107
Stricker, Carrie, 85, 124, 248
Strimmel, Judith C., 248
stroke, 174
Sudanese embassy, 34
Sununu, John, 9, 164–65
Super Bowl, 77
Supreme Court
    decisions, 203, 207, 239
    justices, 190–91, 219, 225
    nominees, 8, 14, 16, 37–41, 43–44, 53, 55, 191–200, 210–17, 222–29, 241, 246
surveillance program, 233, 241, 246

Talent, Jim, 189
Tauzin, Billy, 4–6, 137
tax cuts, 16
Taylor, Bettilou, 109–10
Teamsters Union, conviction of officials, 244
Texas Bar Association, 225
Thomas, Clarence, 8, 40, 45, 223, 245
Thomas, Craig, 47
Thomas Jefferson University Hospital, 26, 60–61, 79, 80, 81, 90, 98–99, 111
Thornburgh v. American College of Obstetricians and Gynecologists, 230
Thurmond, Strom, 62
thyroid cancer, 75
Title IX, 217
Toomey, Patrick J., 10–15, 25–27, 29–30, 34, 35, 36, 42, 58, 220
torture, 69–70
tracheotomy, 75
Tushnet, Mark, 204
Twain, Mark, 117

two-party system, 58
Tyson, Mike, 27

UN. *See* United Nations
United Nations (UN), resolutions, 35
United States Agency for International Development (USAID), 242
Urban, David, 24, 101
USAID. *See* United States Agency for International Development
uterine cancer, 177

Veterans Affairs Committee, 24
violence against women, 200
Violence Against Women Act, 203
violent crime, 68, 241
Vitter, David, 48
Voting Rights Act, 241, 246

Wallace, Andy, 147, 158
Walton, Marie, 123, 124
war crimes tribunal, 35, 241
war on cancer, 174, 195, 239, 247
war on terror, 16, 68, 183, 207–8, 241. *See also* Guantanamo Bay; interrogation; Patriot Act; al Qaeda; torture
Warner, John, 49
Warren Commission, 7, 62, 124, 131, 139, 244
Washington Journal, 77
weapons of mass destruction (WMDs), 35, 68
Webster, Daniel, 63
Weicker, Lowell, 9
Weitz, Howard, 97–99, 101, 127
West, Mae, 170
Wilkinson, J. Harvey, 196
Williams, Armstrong, 120
Wilson, Brian, 41
Wilson, Wyndham, 109
"winning ugly," 26–27
WMDs. *See* weapons of mass destruction
workweek, 172
World War I, 129–30
World War II, 36, 130
Worrall, Tom, 103

Yale Law School, 70, 73, 204
Yeakel, Lynn, 8, 33

Zerhouni, Elias, 109, 180
Zucker, Jerry, 181
Zucker, Katie, 181